novum pro

All rights of distribution,
including via film, radio, and television,
photomechanical reproduction,
audio storage media, electronic data storage media,
and the reprinting of portions of text, are reserved.

© 2020 novum publishing

ISBN 978-1-64268-174-1
Translation: Elaine Milman, Tanya Pernet
Editing: Neva Hay
Cover photos: Kinga Wójcicka Greenmorning,
Wolfgang Bayer
Cover design, layout & typesetting: Marion Wotruba
Internal illustrations: Wolfgang Bayer, Andreas Svirak,
Kinga Wójcicka, Markus Guschelbauer, Helmut Mitter,
Ingram Image

www.novumpublishing.com

DISCLAIMER
The information provided in this book should not be taken as medical advice. If you require a medical diagnosis or prescription, or if you are contemplating any major dietary change, please consult a qualified health-care provider. You should always seek an expert medical opinion before making changes in your diet or supplementation regimen.

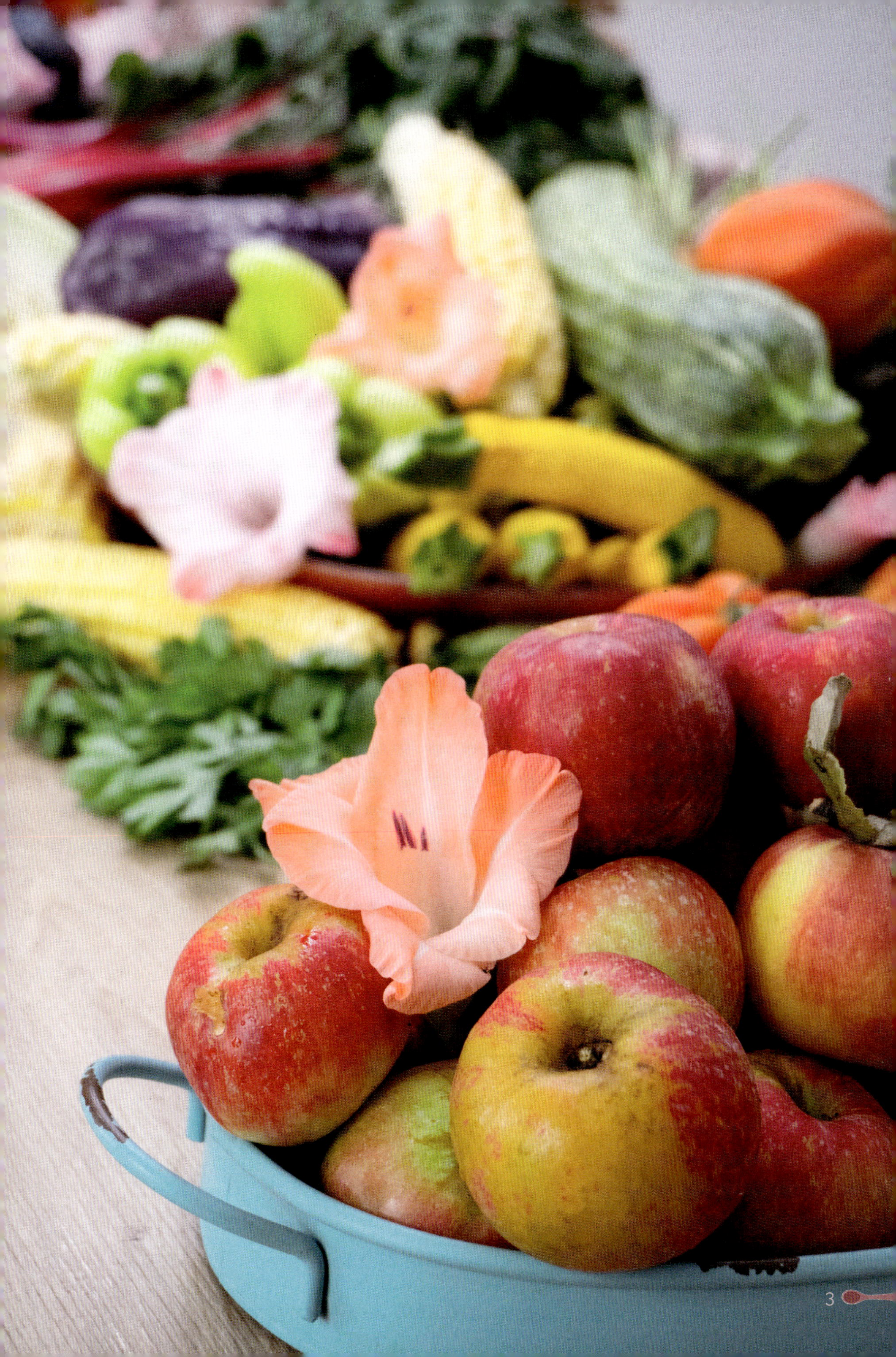

„Om namo bhagavate vasudevaya"

I offer my respectful obeisances to the absolute truth in the all pervading form as Vasudeva, Sri Krishna.

THE QUALITY OF THE FOOD YOU EAT CREATES YOUR STATE OF MIND, EMOTIONS AND CONSCIOUSNESS.

Acknowledgement

I wish to dedicate this cookbook to my parents, Helena and Gojko to express my gratitude for their invaluable love and support. They have raised both my sister and I with high moral values and ignited the light of compassion within us and empathy towards all living creatures.

I also would like to thank my beloved sister, Tanya and her husband Maurice, for their love, support and their motivational words of encouragement.
Thank you, dear Wolfgang Bayer, for your loving support and for your outstanding photography. Also a big thanks to Andreas Svirak, Kinga Wójcicka and Markus Guschelbauer for the many additional gorgeous photos that are included in this cookbook.

My sincere gratitude to dear Elaine Milman, Eva Floigl and Martina Huber for their professionalism in translating this cookbook into English, and Tatjana Pernet and Neva Hay for correcting my manuscript. Also, to Marion Wotruba for her creative beautiful graphic design and illustrations.

Last but not least, I would like to express my biggest gratitude to both my grand spiritual master, A.C. Bhaktivedanta Swami Prabhupada who has selflessly brought the pure wisdom of the Vedas to the western world and to my initiating spiritual master, Sri Rohini Suta Prabhu, who has shown my searching soul its Dharma (path). It is by their mercy that this book is completed.

lokāḥ samastāḥ sukhino bhavantu
"May all beings everywhere be happy and free"

I pray to the Queen of Goddesses, and Divine Cook, Shrimati Radharani, to bestow upon me her mercy, so that my thoughts, words and actions contribute in some way to that happiness and freedom everywhere.

Contents

Acknowledgments ___ 5
Introduction: Ayurveda the Mother of Medicine & Dietetics ___ 12
Healing and spiritual Aspects of Diet & the Science of Taste ___ 16
The seven Ayurveda Constitution Types and recommended Diet ___ 19
A healty Diet for your Constitution ___ 25
Ayurvedic Morning Rituals and Detox ___ 34
Golden Milk (Curcuma Latte) ___ 36
Wise Spices & The Ayurvedic Medicine Chest ___ 40
Ideal Combination of Food ___ 54
Masalas – Spice Mix Powder (Curry-, Garam- and Sambar-Masala) ___ 57
Introduction to Recipes and Yogic Way of Cooking ___ 60

1. BREAKFAST ___ 62
Ayurveda classics (porridge) ___ 65

Cereal Porridge ___ 66
Shredded Cereal Porridge ___ 67
Broccoli and Almond Spread ___ 68
Hummus Chickpea Sesame Spread ___ 69
Smokey Tofu & Sunflower Seed Spread ___ 70
Paneer Curry Herb Spread ___ 71
Avocado-Pumpkin Seed and Basil Spread ___ 72
Brown or Green Lentil Tahini Spread ___ 73

2. SOUPS ___ 74
For the soul ___ 77

Red Lentil Cauliflower Soup ___ 78
Root Vegetables Cream Soup ___ 79
Mung Dal Barley Vegetable Soup ___ 80
Quinoa Vegetable Soup ___ 81
Red Beet and Potato Dill Soup ___ 82
White Beans and Celery Tomato Soup ___ 83
Root Vegetables and Ginger Soup ___ 84
Vegetable Coconut Milk Soup with Sweet Potatoes & Lime Leaves ___ 85
Delicate Red Vegetable Soup "Borscht" ___ 86
Hokkaido Pumpkin Mung Dal Cream Soup ___ 87

3. AHIMSA DAIRY PRODUCTS ___ 88
Ahimsa dairy products ___ 90

Ghee - Ayurvedic Gold (clarified butter) ___ 92
Yoghurt ___ 93
Paneer (White Curd Cheese) ___ 94

4. RICE DISHES — 96
A small grain with a big impact — 99

- Basmati Rice Natural — 100
- Lemon Basmati Rice — 100
- Push Panna (Flower Rice with Nuts and Vegetables) — 101
- Spicy Basmati Rice with Grilled Eggplant and Roasted Cashew Nuts — 102
- Rice with Tomatoes, Peppers and Pine Nuts — 103
- Saffron Rice with Almonds and Sugar Snap Peas — 104
- Sesame Rice with Green Beans, Carrots and Tofu (natural or smoked) — 105
- Basmati Rice Pulao with Cauliflower and Yoghurt Masala — 106
- Brown Rice with Brown Lentils and Vegetables — 107

5. LENTILS AND LEGUMES — 108
A small, round source of high-quality protein — 110

- Alu Chana Dal (split chickpeas - Lentils with Potatoes) — 113
- Warm Lentil Vegetable Salad — 114
- Sambar Dal - Stove Vegetable Stew — 115
- Moussaka - Potato-Eggplant and Lentil Casserole — 116
- Ayurvedic classics - Kitchari rice, dal and vegetable stew — 118
- Kitchari 1 - with colored Vegetables — 119
- Kitchari 2 - with Spinach and Potatoes — 120
- Kitchari 3 - Pulao Rice, Dal and Vegetables from the Wok — 121

6. SUBJIS: CURRIES AND VEGETABLE DISHES — 122
Cooked, steamed, stir-fried — 125

- Colorful Vegetables in Coconut Milk Subji — 126
- Okra Bell Pepper Subji with black Mustard Seeds — 127
- Green Beans, Carrot and Pepper Subji — 128
- Sweet Potato, Spinach and Paneer Subji — 129
- Spicy Potato Nut Stew — 131
- Glazed Colorful Vegetables from the Wok with Tofu and Soy Sauce — 132
- Cauliflower and Potato Subji — 135
- Baked Beetroot with Potatoes and Cauliflower in Herb-Nigella Seeds-Sauce — 135
- Oven-baked Vegetable Curry in Tagine (Morocan cooking vessel) — 137
- Creamy Spinach, Eggplant and Yellow Lentils — 139
- Zucchini, Potato and Pepper Subji — 140
- Potato Paneer Gratin „Gauranga" — 141
- Fennel, Potatoes and Mangold (Chard) in Coconut Milk Subji with Homemade Cheese Paneer — 141
- Oven-baked Vegetable Curry — 142
- Green Beans, Carrots and Potatoes in a delicious Kadhy Sauce — 143

7. FLATBREADS 144
Simple or filled – always a highlight 146

Chapati - griddle-baked Bread (flat Bread without Yeast) 147
Aloo Patra - Spicy Potato Spelt Roulade with grated Coconut, Lemon and Ajwain Seeds 149
Bhatura with Black Pepper and Coriander (Griddle-Fried Plain Flatbread with Baking Soda) 150
Paneer Paratha filled with Paneer (Homemade Cheese) or Feta 151
Aloo Paratha - Puff Flatbread with Potato Filling 152
Dal Katchori - Flatbread filled with spicy Dal 155
Samosas - Filled Pastries 156
Aloo Gobi Samosa stuffed Dumplings with Cauliflower and Potatoes (baked in the oven) 157
Spinach Potato Samosas 158

8. SNACKS, PATTIES, CASSEROLES & PILAFS 160
Add a salad for a full meal 163

Potato and Coriander Patties in Coconut Crackling 167
Millet Chickpea Pulao with Vegetables 169
Simple Swiss Potato Patties „Roesties" 170
Chickpea Nuggets with Buckwheat 171
Green Spelt Marjoram Patties 172
Millet and Carrot Patties 173
Carrot and Coconut Chickpea Vada (fried Patties) 174
Cauliflower Kofta „Gobi Kofta"
(Fried Balls from Cauliflower and Chickpea Flour) 175
Pudla - Patties made with Chickpea Flour and Vegetables 176
Uppma (Hearty Vegetable Spelt Semolina Stew) 177
Ayurvedic Lasagna with Eggplant and Zucchini 178
Idli - Spicy Dal Cereal Dumplings 179
„Pakora" Fried Vegetables in Chickpea Dough 181
Cabbage Kofta (Deep-fried Balls) 181

9. CHUTNEYS 182
Fruity spicy sauces 184

Apple and Ginger Chutney 185
Caramel Banana Almond Chutney 186
Mango Mint Chutney 186
Apricot Chutney 187
Plum Chutney 188
Peach or Nectarine Chutney 189
Coconut Yoghurt Dal Chutney 189

10. SALADS AND RAITAS ... 190
Raw vegetables for lunch ... 193

- Warm Vegetable Salad ... 195
- Summer Rice Salad with Kalamata Olives, Feta Cheese & Vegetables ... 196
- Noodle Avocado Chickpea Salad ... 199
- Waldorf Salad ... 200
- Arugula Tofu and Tomato Salad ... 200
- Young Cabbage and Lamb's Lettuce Salad with Avocado ... 201
- Potato Coconut Raita ... 202
- Endive Potato Pumpkin Seed Salad ... 203
- Eggplant (Aubergine) and Walnut Raita ... 204
- Mint Raita ... 205
- Tasty and Delicate Banana Raita with Cilantro ... 205
- Yellow Lentil Raita ... 206
- Cucumber and Carrot Raita ... 207

11. DESSERTS ... 208
A little sweetness that you can enjoy with a good conscience ... 211

- Brownies (sugar-free) ... 212
- Energy Balls ... 213
- Saffron Halava ... 214
- Caramel and Semolina Halava ... 215
- (not the same as Middle Eastern Candy "Halvah")
- Mango Mascarpone Cake ... 216
- Besan Laddu ... 217
- (Sweets made with chickpea flour)
- Delicious Apple Cake without Dough ... 218
- Carrot Almonds Halava ... 219
- Coconut Pancakes without Eggs ... 219
- Apple Jelly Cake with whipped Cream ... 220
- Shrikand - Thick Yoghurt with Saffron and Orange Zest ... 222
- Plum Lemon Cardamom Cake ... 223
- Chocolate Nut Cherry Jam Balls ... 224
- Apple Ricotta Pie ... 225
- Almond Rice Cardamom Pudding ... 226
- Tapioca Cardamom Pudding with Coconut Milk ... 227
- Nankhatai (Ayurvedic Cookies) ... 229
- Banana Bread (sugar-free) ... 229

12. Drinks ... 230
Warm in the winter and refreshing in the summer. ... 232

- Refreshing Ginger-Apple Drink ... 232
- Fruity Coconut Milk ... 232

Lime Rose Drink	233
Saffron Lemonade	235
Veda Punch	235
Homemade Yogi Tea - Chai	236
Hot Evening Milk with Pistachios and Raisins	237
Ginger Orange Tea	237
Veda-Cola with Tamarind	238
Mango Lassi	238
Salty Lassi with Mint	238
Salty Lassi Drink with Cumin	239
Lemon Honey Drink	239
Almond Milk	239

13. HEALTHY GUT - HAPPY LIFE — 240
Intestinal Health — 242

Sauerkraut	243
Reed Beet "Kwass"	244
Buckwheat Rice Bread (natural Fermentation with Sourdough)	245
Carob-Buckwheat Cake	246
Apple-Carrot-Almond Cake	247
Check-List	248

About the author — 250

Ayurveda – the mother of medicine

Ayurveda literally means "the science of a long and healthy life" and is a thousand-year-old medicine of ancient India.

Ayurveda is a holistic science of health and medicine which sees the human being as an entity of body, spirit and soul. As a life's guidebook, it also offers different forms of therapies that can remove human diseases and suffering. Ayurvedic forms of therapy include: nutrition, herbalism, meditation, yoga, the singing of mantras, behavioural therapy, gemstone therapy, music therapy and spiritual therapy.

The origin of Ayurveda lies in the Vedic advanced civilisation which dates back presumably 5,000 to 7,000 years. The founders of Ayurveda are called Rishis. Rishi is a Vedic term for remarkable ancient sages and spiritual scientists with divine knowledge. Vedic tradition regards the rishis as "great sadhus" or "sages" who after intense meditation (tapas) realized the Supreme Truth and eternal knowledge, which they composed into hymns.

Sri Dhanvantari, one of the many incarnations of Krishna and Vishnu, is the founder and patron saint of Ayurveda. Initially, the medical science was passed on orally. The first written records in Sanskrit are about 5,000 years old. The most important and still-existing Ayurveda scriptures are Charaka Samhita, Sushruta Samhita and Ashtanga Samgraha.

AYURVEDIC DIETETICS

Ayurveda offers advice for nutrition and diet to prevent illness and increase resistance to disease. Many reasons for illness and discomfort can be found in a wrong diet. Furthermore, what we eat also affects our feelings. According to Ayurveda, different food will affect us physically and emotionally in positive or negative ways.

According to Ayurveda, we should change our diet for the purpose of long-term health. The following factors influence the effect of food:

- quality of food
- preparation
- combination
- quantity
- origin
- season of the year and time of the day
- consciousness during cooking and eating

> Just like Universe, body, too, consists of five elements. Pancamahabhuta or five great elements are the basis of life of the whole universe (the macrocosm), as well as our body (the microcosm), and are known as the five great elements: space/ether (ākāśa); air/wind (vāyu); fire (tejas); water (jala); earth (pṛthvī). In Ayurvedic philosophy, the five elements combine in pairs to form three dynamic

forces or interactions called Dosha. Derived from the Pancamahabhutas, each Dosha which cannot be detected with our senses but their qualities – is a combination of any two of the five Bhutas with the predominance of one. Called Vata, Pitta and Kapha in Sanskrit, these three are responsible for all the physiological and psychological processes within the body and mind – dynamic forces that determine growth and decay. Every physical characteristic, mental capacity and the emotional tendency of a human being can therefore be explained in terms of the Tridoshas.

VATA
Vata represents movement, transport, sensory functions and the ability to communicate. All body functions are governed by Vata.

PITTA
Pitta is responsible for the metabolism, digestion, regulation of body heat, temperature, intellect and emotional expression.

KAPHA
Kapha controls the fluid balance of the body and immune resistance. Cohesion, structure and stability also depend on Kapha.

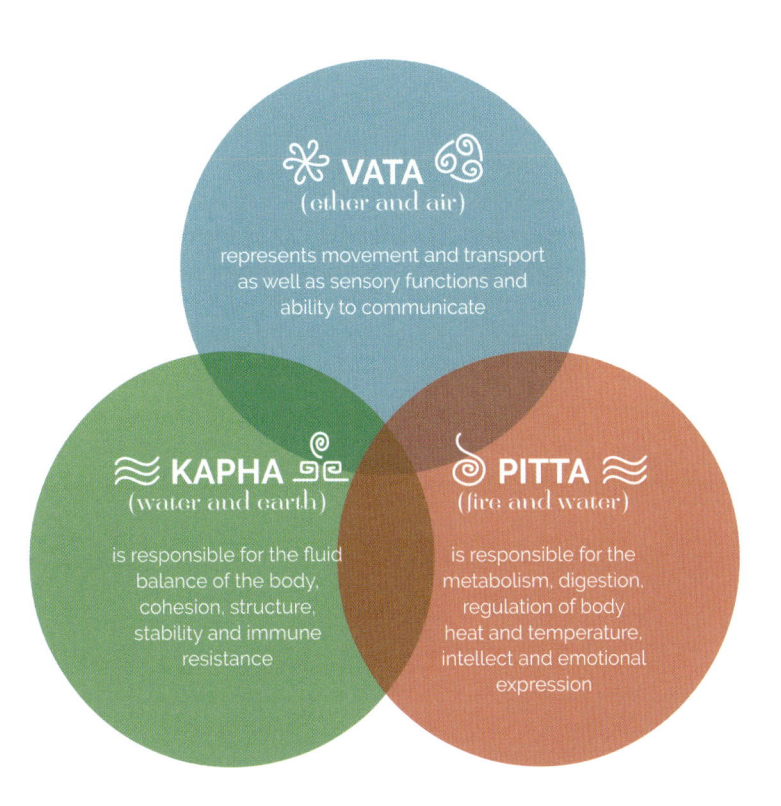

VATA (ether and air)
represents movement and transport as well as sensory functions and ability to communicate

KAPHA (water and earth)
is responsible for the fluid balance of the body, cohesion, structure, stability and immune resistance

PITTA (fire and water)
is responsible for the metabolism, digestion, regulation of body heat and temperature, intellect and emotional expression

Ojas – vital energy

There is not only a direct connection between the food you eat and your health, but food affects your happiness as well. Health and happiness have a common source in a single product of digestion — called ojas.
Ojas is the physical equivalent of both bliss and immunity. It is what causes the eyes to sparkle, the skin to look radiant and the immunity to be strong. And it's directly related to digestion.
Ojas is the finest and most refined product of digestion and metabolism.

"The whitish to orange-red fluid that is based in the heart is called Ojas (vital essence). When Ojas is lost, the man dies."
"Ojas is the first thing created in the body of all living beings. It has the colour of melted butter, tastes like honey and smells like puffed rice."
Charaka Samhita

In Ayurvedic dietetics, Ojas is the term for vital energy. As honey is the essence of nectar, Ojas is the essence of the body tissue. Ojas influences human immune resistance, makes you feel blissful and gives a bright look and inner beauty. There are two kinds of Ojas:

Param Ojas (8 drops; the loss of Param Ojas will lead to death)
Aparam Ojas (a handful; non-fatal when it is reduced)

Agni – the digestive fire

"All diseases are caused by an imbalance of Agni."

Agni is the cosmic principle of transformation. In our body in the digestive system, Agni is responsible for breaking down and absorbing the food we have been eating and converting it into body tissue. Jatharagni, the central digestive fire, is situated in the lower stomach and upper part of the small intestine, where the most important digestive processes are taking place. If our Agni is strong, we feel full of energy, healthy and a sense of well-being. On the other hand, if our Agni is weak, our body will not digest well, creating Ama (toxins) – the preliminary stage of all diseases.

Ama – toxic residue

Literally translated, Ama means "undigested" or "half-cooked". Ama is metabolic waste products which accumulate in the body and can cause diseases when they are not excreted. Ama clogs the channels of the body, preventing nutrients from being delivered efficiently to the cells and preventing wastes from being discharged from the body.

There are various symptoms for Ama in the body:

- indigestion
- fatigue
- depression
- lack of energy
- susceptibility to infections
- stiffness
- increased salivation
- coated tongue
- acrid and strong smell of perspiration
- bad and slow wound healing
- skin rash, itching
- swollen eyes and lymph nodes

How can Ama be reduced?
Drink "Ama Pachana" Spice Water throughout the day:
Mix the following spices together: cumin seeds, fennel seeds, peppercorns, anise seeds, and mint. Make a tea with 1 tsp. of the spices, two thin slices of fresh ginger, and 300 ml boiling water.

Panchakarma – the ultimate and most effective healing experience in the science of Ayurveda.

"Panchakarma" is the most famous detoxification process of Ayurveda, restoring youth with the help of medicated oils. Panchakarma, which literally means 'five detox processes' in Sanskrit, is a transformative ayurvedic therapy to remove toxins and to restore the natural constitution of body and mind.

Every single day, our body accumulates various kinds of toxins from food, drinks, environment etc. This toxic accumulation, known as Ama in Ayurveda, disturbs the natural biochemistry and functioning of all organs within the body. Over the years, the toxins in the body blocks the flow of Prana (vital energy) which causes imbalance in the five elements and three Dosha constitution of our body, and mind too.

Customized for each individual patient, Panchakarma procedures follow a specific program of treatments that result in purification, rejuvenation and regeneration. Diet, ayurvedic herbal medicines, yoga and meditations facilitate the healing and regeneration processes.

Healing and spiritual aspects of diet & the science of taste

The effects of the six tastes (rasas)
According to Ayurveda, there are six different tastes which, in abundance, raise or lower the three Doshas. The six tastes should be balanced nutritionally in the diet for optimum health. The Ayurvedic principle of the six tastes is the key in the science of Ayurvedic herbal formulation as well.

SWEET (MADHURA)
(milk, butter, grains, sweet potatoes, rice, pasta, honey, sugar, sweetener, ripe fruit, dried fruit, root vegetables, nuts, seeds)

SOUR (AMLA)
(citrus fruits, tomatoes, yoghurt, vinegar, tamarind)

SALTY (LAVANA)
(sea salt, rock salt, black salt and soy sauce)

PUNGENT & HOT (KATU)
(fresh herbs, cress, mustard, spices such as: ginger, chili, paprika, pepper, cinnamon, cloves, cardamom, nigella seeds)

BITTER (TIKTA)
(all green vegetables like leafy greens, cabbage, broccoli, kale, salad, herbs, asparagus, bitter gourd, vermouth, barley, aloe vera and spices such as: turmeric, fenugreek, asafoetida)

ASTRINGENT (KASHAI)
(all legumes like lentils and beans, berries, apple, pear, quince, spinach, aubergines, artichokes, yoghurt, black tea and herbal tea, pomegranate (tastes sour on the tongue but is both astringent and bitter), quinoa and sprouts

Sweet, sour and salty tastes increase Kapha and reduces Vata. Sour, salty and pungent tastes increase Pitta. Sweet, bitter and astringent tastes reduce Pitta. Pungent, bitter and astringent tastes increase Vata and reduce Kapha.

> Try to include some lentils, bitter and astringent foods in your daily diet. An easy way to do it is to add turmeric and fenugreek seeds to your foods as they are cooking. You can sauté them in ghee and then add to your vegetables. Turmeric is both bitter and astringent. It is considered a blood purifier and an antioxidant. Curcumin in turmeric and piperine in black pepper have been shown to improve health due to their anti-inflammatory, antioxidant and disease-fighting qualities.

The three Gunas – modes of nature

The Upanishads, the most ancient scriptures in India, speak of food as "Brahman", the divine. The entity or unity of all life shows in the process of eating, through which we are participating in the creation of the material world.

A healthy diet alone cannot be enough to completely cure diseases. Still, the right diet will help to mitigate illness and pain (suffering) and gain balance and well-being. According to Ayurveda, food has a therapeutic effect on the human body that can be enhanced by particular food preparation with the right spices and fats.

Ayurveda teaches us that all that exists is determined by the three Gunas or modes of nature: Tamas, Rajas and Sattva. Regarding diet, three different forms of diet derive from the three Gunas:

Tamas is the principle of dullness, darkness and resistance. Tamas food is passive. It increases qualities such as ignorance, greed, laziness, foolishness, depression and despair. Food of this kind requires a lot of energy to digest and does not have any vital energy. Tamas food is food with bad smell and taste, old, rotten, sterilised, cold, or stale food. This includes meat, fish, eggs, peanuts, mushrooms, homogenised milk, hard cheese, fast food, canned food and frozen food. Tamas food should be avoided.

Rajas is the principle of energy, activity, emotion, turbulence and passion. Rajas food causes hyperactivity, restlessness, irritability, aggression, insomnia, unclear complexion, raises blood pressure and increases toxins in the blood. Rajas food is very pungent, very salty, very sour, hot or dry food, for example, coffee, chocolate, alcohol, energy drinks, onion, garlic, fish, ketchup, beer, wine, deep-fried food, preservatives or industrially processed food.

Sattva is the principle of light, awareness, intelligence, harmony, virtue and clarity. Such food of immaculate quality increases consciousness, emotional harmony and does not contain any pathogenic factors. Food of Sattva quality includes fresh milk and dairy products from happy cows (ahimsa milk products where the cows are not slaughtered), grains (especially wheat and rice), fruit, vegetables, lentils and beans, ghee (clarified butter), nuts, seeds and herbs. Sattva food is fresh, juicy, oily, nourishing and sweet. A Sattvic diet contains a high amount of energy and has a positive karmic impact.

The Sattvic diet goes back to Bhakti yogis. Bhakti yogis were practising yoga and completely consecrating themselves to the Divine. This kind of diet is especially important for people who focus on their intellect, because it nurtures intellectual qualities and energy. A person will be able to advance in a spiritual way or increase the level of consciousness only with a Sattvic diet.

Prasadam – spiritualised, holy food

A lacto-vegetarian diet comes closest to a diet following the Sattva principle and is the perfect diet for body, spirit and soul. Of course, it has to be adopted individually and according to time, place and circumstances.

The Sattvic diet and Bhagavad-Gita also recommends to bless our daily food. We should try to carry out all of our activities with gratitude and love and dedicate them to the Divine. This principle can be applied to all spheres of life, including our daily food. As God provides us with food through his creation, everything that we eat should first be offered to the creator with love and devotion (Bhakti). For example, you can make a little prayer, speak a mantra, or perform a ritual of gratitude which can be found in every religion.

Lord Krishna says in the Bhagavad-Gita:
(chapter 9, verse 26)

"Patram puhspam phalam toyam yo me bhaktya prayacchati. Tad aham bhakti-upahritam ashnami praya-tatmanaha."
(If someone offers me a leaf, a flower, a fruit or some water with love and devotion, I will accept it.)

Offering prayer mantra:
"om namo bhagavate vasudevaya"
(With due respect, I pay homage to the absolute truth in its all-pervading form as Vasudeva Krishna.)

"Lord Krishna" painted by Syamarani dd
www.bhaktiart.net

SACRED CONSCIOUSNESS OF FOOD OR HOW FOOD CAN INCREASE YOUR AWARENESS OF LIFE

The cook should be aware that the alchemical power of cooking which affects the food and therefore should handle the foods with consciousness and care. The kitchen should be clean and also the cook should be freshly showered. Meditation & mantra music or classic music playing in the background helps to concentrate on the process of cooking. During cooking, do not taste the food, as it will disturb your digestion. After some time, you will learn how to taste with your other senses like eyes and intuition. This is a powerful process of developing self-confidence. Eat the spiritualized food only after you put the food on the table and have spoken a prayer or mantra. This is called cooking as meditation and alchemy – simple foods will be transformed into remedies.

THE SEVEN AYURVEDA CONSTITUTION TYPES AND RECOMMENDED DIET

In Ayurveda, the constitution (mind-body state) or Prakriti of a person decides the methods and means of preventive health care, diet and therapy.

There are seven different Prakritis (constitution types):

- Vata
- Pitta
- Kapha
- Vata/Pitta
- Vata/Kapha
- Pitta/Kapha
- Vata/Pitta/Kapha

According to Ayurveda, your mind-body constitution is determined by the individual distribution of the three Doshas with which you are born. Like your whole life, your individual constitution is dynamic and goes through different changes, for example, in different seasons, different periods of life, or periods of stress. It is important that you get to know your own unique nature so that you can live according to it.

DISCOVER YOUR DOSHA TYPE!

The following chart will help you to determine your mind-body constitution. For every question, you will find three different attributes. Check the attribute that you find is most applicable to you. If you find two attributes are describing your personality, mark them both.

Finally, add up the number of checks. The principle (or Dosha) that received the highest number of checks is the most predominant force. For example, when you have 24 points for Vata, 13 for Pitta and 5 for Kapha, you are a Vata type.

If you have nearly the same number of checks for two Doshas, you are a mixed type. For example, when you have 16 points for Vata, 5 for Pitta and 15 for Kapha, you are a Vata/Kapha type.

If all three Doshas are nearly the same, you are a Tridosha type. For example, 12 points for Vata, 11 for Pitta and 13 for Kapha.

Constitution chart

	✻ VATA ൦	◐ PITTA ≈	≈ KAPHA ൦
appearance	thin, slender, lanky, with prominent bones and joints	medium build, sporty, energetic	corpulent, large, round, well-proportioned, high fat content
skin	thin (visible veins), dry, rough	warm, moist, soft, smooth, freckles, moles, wrinkled	thick, cold, moist, soft, smooth
complexion	dark brown, dull	pink, yellow, reddish	white, bright
hair	brown, dark but not black, dry, rough	fair or very fair, fine, hair loss, turning grey rapidly	black, curly, greasy, thick, oily
face	prominent cheekbones, small restless eyes, fine lips, small, uneven teeth	prominent nose, saggy skin, wrinkles, reddened eyes, red lips, a tendency towards herpes and stomatitis	attractive, broad, large pleasant eyes, beautiful full lips, big beautiful teeth
shoulders	small	medium	broad
chest	thin	medium	strong
arms	thin, prominent bones and veins	medium	long, big, strong
hands	cold, dry, raw, chapped	warm, moist, rosy	cool, thick, large, firm
legs	thin, prominent joints	medium	thick, strong, firm
feet	cold, small	medium	cold, thick, large
joints	thin, small, cracking noises	medium, loose, flexible, soft	thick, large, do not crack
nails	small, dry	soft, rosy	thick, large, smooth, white
appetite	irregular	strong, very thirsty	little, but loves food
stool	hard, dry, constipation, flatulence	large amount, soft, sometimes diarrhea	oily, average shape, mucous in stool
urine	little, occasionally, sometimes with difficulty	excessive, yellow, strong smell, sour	little
sweat	little, no smell	excessive, strong smell	little
voice	weak, throaty, broken, stuttering	sharp, clear	deep, melodic

speech	quick, speaks a lot, changes topics frequently	excellent speaker, fluent, argumentative, convincing	slow, determined, sticks to the topic
strength	weak	difficult to restrain	very strong
immune resistance	low	average	high
walk/gait	quick, restless	not recognizable	slow, steady
behaviour	artistic, often falls in love and changes partners, sometimes jealous, not religious, begins many different things but does not finish them, sensitive	gets angry quickly but also gets happy quickly, kind but does not tolerate misbehaviour, humorous, analytical, targeted, ambitious, competitive, stubborn, determined	patient, tolerant, contented, considerate, conscientious, steady, religious, emphatic, calm, faithful, generous
emotions	worried, anxious, short-tempered, emotionally unstable, imaginative power	angry, impulsive, impatient, critical	calm, tolerant, mature, serious, dependable, stable, composed
intelligence	average, quick wit	excellent, quick wit	good, slow to comprehend
memory	bad, forgetful	good	excellent
sleep pattern	less than 6 hours/day, difficulties to fall asleep, a tendency to awaken easily, gnashing of teeth	6 – 8 hours average	at least 8 hours/day or more
dreams	flying, climbing, nightmares	fire, lightning, gold, sun, flowers, many colours	waters, nature, paradise, relaxation
hobbies	music, poetry, reading, travelling, dancing, chatting	politics, sports, hunting, fighting, debating	reading, hiking, water sports
sensitivities	sensitive to cold and wind	sensitive to heat and sun	sensitive to cold
diseases	mental illness and pain	fever, inflammation	overweight, mucous congestion, diabetes, arteriosclerosis
relationship	often changing, very few friends	friends and enemies	good, strong and stable friendships
offspring	not more than one child	up to two children	more than two children
prosperity	little, few possessions	average	large or working towards a prosperous life, many possessions, wealth
points:	**Vata:**	**Pitta:**	**Kapha:**

VATA TYPE

Vata types are slim and either tall or extremely small. Typical characteristics are long, slim hands, prominent facial features and cracking joints. Their hair is rather brittle and dry. Vata refers to highly sensitive people, sometimes shy and creative, intuitive and perceptive by nature. They are easily excited and quick-acting, but also easily exhausted.

Routine jobs are not suitable for Vata types as they adore change, are artistic, and demonstrate a positive attitude towards new things. Vata types are adventurous and fond of traveling. They often change partners, work or education. People with this constitution are often restless and nervous. They react sensitively to influences of their environment such as noises, cold, wind, change of weather or negative energy.

Vata types also have a very irregular appetite. Sometimes they eat little or wholly refrain from food and sometimes they eat a lot and heartily. Vata types often suffer from constipation and dry stools.

Their skin is mostly dry and they do not appreciate cold at all. Vata types prefer to stay in the sun the whole day.

Being able to evolve in their profession is important for this type of Dosha. Vata types are apt to be involved with creative and artistic tasks and are particularly suitable for teaching and the healing professions.

They need relaxation, harmony, regularity and warmth. Vata types need dishes with sweet, sour or salty flavours. A Vata type diet ought to be nutritious, relaxing and earthy. It should contain dishes that are warm, heavy, strengthening, mildly seasoned and liquid.

PITTA TYPE

Pitta types are rather harmonically proportioned. They are of medium height and have sensitive skin with freckles as well as silky, thin hair that turns grey early. Men often go bald.

They are intense, quick and irritable. Pitta types are critical, ambitious and motivated people who easily reach their goals. Pitta types are born fighters and workaholics. Due to their quick-wittedness, they act faster than other people and they are prone to impatience. They cannot bear heat as they need the cold in order to cool down their hot temper.

Pitta types love eating and drinking. They are hardly able to skip a meal as their inner "digesting fire" constantly burns and asks for replenishment. They cannot tolerate criticism. Pitta types can often be found in scientific professions or leadership positions. They have charisma and the ability to convince others. Successful managers, politicians or self-employed people often have a Pitta constitution.

Meat, fish, eggs, or sour or salty tastes are harmful to Pitta persons. As these foods increase their bodies' inner heat, they should eat sweet, bitter and astringent foods which have a cooling effect on their body which then calms their hot temper.

KAPHA TYPE

Kapha constitutions are compact, sturdy and strong. They have broad shoulders and hands, a strong chest, big eyes, nose and lips and beautiful, big, white teeth. Their hair is dense and strong and their voice is beautiful and low. Kapha persons are very patient, down-to-earth, calm and compassionate.

For them, food is a pleasure, a kind of emotional satisfaction. Comfort, security and a certain amount of affluence are important for them. It always takes Kapha persons a little longer to understand and to act. However, their decisions are indeed reasonable. They think conservatively and are skeptical of changes, which makes Kapha persons slightly slower. Nevertheless, they are balanced, stable and satisfied.

Kapha persons are often found in professions that provide stability and routine, such as in administration, politics, nursing, education or agriculture. They are faithful partners who hardly get involved with adventures. Kapha persons ought to avoid heavy, hearty, oily and sweet dishes. Flavours, such as hot, bitter and astringent are ideal for Kapha persons.

VATA/PITTA TYPE

Vata/Pitta types are pure action. Air matched with fire equals even more disturbance, change, worries, ideas and hyperactivity. They are intelligent and sensitive people. Vata and Pitta influences often alternate. In a harmonious condition, Vata and Pitta persons unite Vata's flexibility and inventiveness with Pitta's pragmatic and purposeful ability to implement.

They love the sun and warmth but avoid strong heat. Pitta allows them to eat a lot and well, but they hardly gain weight. They have digestive problems, which is caused by Vata. Vata/Pitta constitutions often complain about sleep disorders, headaches and a sensitive stomach.

They need stability and regularity. Because carbohydrates are grounding, it is ideal for such types. If you tend to have a stronger Vata part, you should stick to the rules of the Vata diet. If the Pitta type is more prominent, you should stick to the recommendations for a Pitta diet.

Dishes should be seasoned only slightly, not hot, but tranquilizing and stabilizing. For lunch, particularly in summer, they can eat plenty of raw food. In winter, healthy sweets made with dates and cereals should be on the daily menu.

VATA/KAPHA TYPE

Vata/Kapha types unite two contrary doshas. Cold is the only common characteristic of Vata and Kapha. Therefore such types need a lot of warmth, on a bodily, but also on an emotional level.

Vata/Kapha constitutions have a loving and calm manner. That is why we often find such people in healing, psychological and pastoral professions. They are often too weak to say "no". Outwardly people of such type seem sociable. Inwardly they only allow a few people to come nearer.

They take a stand for things with heart and soul. They do not see their limits and tend to overdo it.

A Vata/Kapha person's height is often above average. They, in particular, need a lot of warmth, affection and love.

The flavours sour, salty and hot do them good. Ideally, they should eat a lot of vegetables with stimulating and warming spices. Dinner should be a light meal for Vata/Kapha constitutions. Fried, heavy and oily food as well as big portions ought to be avoided.

PITTA/KAPHA TYPE

Pitta/Kapha persons are of rounded build and medium height. The active metabolism of Pitta and the resilient constitution of Kapha guarantee good health if you combine a lot of exercise with moderate eating.

For these persons, the stability and endurance of Kapha meets the effectiveness and power of Pitta. It is not a coincidence that they are often rather successful people. Pitta/Kapha persons are committed, social and loving. They have their own perception of the world and do not follow well-intended advice.

Their flavors are bitter and astringent. All bitter types of vegetables (green ones and leafy vegetables), plenty of crudités for lunch and legumes five times a week are ideal. Very salty and oily food can cause skin blemishes and irritations. Coriander, saffron and basil have a balancing effect on Pitta/Kapha constitutions.

VATA/PITTA/KAPHA TYPE
TRIDOSHA

Vata/Pitta/Kapha types or Tridoshas are harder to find than the other constitutions. These persons are very balanced and have a maximum resilience against illnesses as they were born with a natural inner equilibrium.

A balanced, lacto-vegetarian diet that takes the seasons into account preserves these dosha's balance and, therefore, their optimal health. One-sidedness is to be avoided. All flavors can be enjoyed in moderation. A Tridosha type should comply with the general Ayurvedic nutrition guidelines.

> **A HEALTHY DIET FOR YOUR CONSTITUTION**
>
> I refrained from mentioning meat, fish and eggs in my recommendation. I believe that these foods are not beneficial for human health. This does not mean that Ayurveda forbids these foods. Every person should decide individually which diet he or she can reconcile with his or her conscience. However, Ayurveda clearly suggests a balanced lacto-vegetarian diet.

Vata reducing diet

People with Vata constitutions should consume sweet, sour, salty, liquid, warming, moist and nutritious dishes. They should eat three times a day at regular times. Vata types should not fast longer than one day. Light soups are particularly suitable for fasting as Vata types need to be provided with enough liquid. Food should always be freshly prepared and with a lot of love since Vata persons are highly sensitive and can easily experience digestive disorder.

For breakfast, spelt or kamut porridge with steamed fruits, a dash of cream, raw sugar and warming spices such as cinnamon, cardamom, ginger or anise are particularly suitable. Coffee or hot chocolate are not beneficial as they have an artificially stimulating effect. Alternatively, grain coffee with milk can be tried. Depending on the season, nuts, lassi or chai can be part of a snack. For lunch, one can have rice with vegetables, a bit of mung dal with a spoonful of yogurt and a little dessert.

Vata persons with a healthy digestion can occasionally enjoy a piece of cake with a cup of tea or grain coffee. For dinner, soup made of root vegetables is recommended. Another possibility are one or two pieces of toast (warm) with a vegetarian spread, warm pasta with pesto, couscous vegetable pilaf or a warm bulgur stir fry. When preparing these meals, flatulence-inhibiting spices and a high-quality fat such as ghee or sesame oil should be used.

Vata natures often suffer from food allergies, digestive disorders, sleeping problems, rheumatic illnesses, nerve problems and painful menstruation. Ideal food supplements: Chyavanprash, Ashwagandha, Brahmi, Triphala ("the three fruits": Amalaki, Haritaki and Bibhitaki; bowel tonic and mild laxative).

FOODS FOR VATA CONSTITUTIONS:

VEGETABLES
Vegetables are well-tolerated by Vata persons, especially when prepared with sufficient ghee, butter, cream or oil.

Ideal: carrots, parsnip, sweet potatoes, beetroot, okra, green beans, celery, avocado, yam, eggplant, pumpkin, cucumber, few tomatoes, sprouts
Less recommended: any type of cabbage, peppers, leafy vegetables, mushrooms, bitter salad such as chicory, raw onions

GRAIN
Grain boiled in a lot of water is very good for Vata persons. Dry grains, such as bread or dry cereals, ought to be avoided.

Ideal: spelt, wheat, rice, oats, kamut
Less recommended: corn, rye, buckwheat, barley, quinoa, millet

LEGUMES
Legumes are an ideal protein source. As they are flatulent, they need to be prepared with soothing spices such as cumin, caraway, coriander or asafetida.

Ideal: mung dal, red lentils, urad dal, brown lentils
Less recommended: chickpeas, chana dal, toor dal, tofu, any kind of beans, particularly soya beans

FRUIT
Sweet and slightly sour fruits are good for Vata constitutions. One should only eat them in small amounts or steamed since fruits are rather light and are not grounding. Dried fruits should be soaked overnight and boiled in order to have them in breakfast porridge. This is particularly helpful for constipation.

Ideal: pineapples, strawberries, cherries, plums, raspberries, figs, bananas, mangos, papayas, citrus fruits, peaches, apricots, melons, sweet apples
Less recommended: pear, quince

DAIRY PRODUCTS
Dairy products, particularly fermented ones, are good for Vata persons. Milk should never be drunk cold.

Ideal: ghee, yogurt, whipped cream, kefir, sour cream, cream cheese, curd cheese, milk
Less recommended: buttermilk, hard cheese

FATS AND OILS
Fats and oils are essential for Vata constitutions

Ideal: ghee, sesame oil, coconut oil, pumpkin seed oil, olive oil, sunflower oil
Less recommended: corn oil, soya oil, peanut oil
Not recommended: canola oil, margarine

SWEETENERS
Sweet dishes ought to be an inherent part of a Vata person's diet since they are grounding.

Ideal: dates, jaggery, raw brown sugar, palm sugar, maple syrup, young honey
Less recommended: mature honey
Not recommended: white sugar

SPICES
Spices, particularly when anti-flatulent or appetizing, are especially appropriate for Vata.
Hot and bitter spices are to be avoided.

Ideal: saffron, cardamom, cinnamon, asafetida, ajwain, cumin, coriander, anise, basil, oregano, marjoram, clove, sea and rock salt, fennel, caraway, nutmeg
Less recommended: chili

SEEDS AND NUTS
Slightly roasted seeds and nuts are ideal for Vata persons.

Ideal: almonds, pistachios, sesame, cashews, walnuts, pumpkin seeds, sunflower seeds, flaxseeds, coconut, poppy seeds
Not recommended: peanuts

Pitta reducing diet

Pitta natures should consume sweet, bitter, astringent, nutritious, moist, cooling and mild dishes. However, sour, hot, very salty, warming, oily and dry dishes should be avoided. Fasting is absolutely unsuitable for Pitta persons as their digestion is very strong. They need to constantly replenish the calories that are burned up. If a Pitta type wants to fast, he or she should do it with freshly squeezed juices for one or two days per month maximum. Pitta persons should not skip meals, as they tend to become quite irritable if they do not eat regularly.

A Pitta diet should contain plenty of liquid food. Alcohol ought to be absolutely avoided. Nevertheless, non-alcoholic beer is an ideal Pitta drink as it is cooling and is non-irritating. Coffee can be consumed with milk. Non-carbonated mineral water, milk, fruit juices (except orange or pineapple juice) and herbal teas that are not too hot are ideal.

Pitta persons need a hearty breakfast that ideally consists of rice porridge with mild spices such as cardamom, fennel and anise or spelt bread with various vegetarian spreads. The first coffee in the morning should by all means be consumed after 10:00 a.m. since the body should de-acidify early in the morning. Instead of bean coffee, one can use grain coffee or malt coffee.

For lunch, a lot of raw food (bitter salads such as endives or radicchio) along with steamed leafy and green vegetables (spinach, chard, savoy cabbage, broccoli, zucchini, fennel, okra) is ideal. It can be combined with coconut milk sauce, rice with mung dal, chickpeas or dill potatoes. Pitta persons do not need to skip dessert. However, fried or heavily oily food should be avoided. In the afternoon, herbal or chai tea is suitable.

Potato soup or minestrone is a perfect dinner. It is important to avoid hard cheese or sausage in the evening as they cause acid in the body. Rice pilaf with vegetables or pasta is also appropriate for a Pitta dinner.

Pitta persons often suffer from problems such as acne, abscesses, skin blemishes as well as liver, spleen and gall bladder disorders, inflammations, gastritis and high blood pressure.

Ideal food supplements are: evening primrose oil, Triphala, Chyavanprash

FOODS FOR PITTA CONSTITUTIONS

VEGETABLES
Pitta types can handle raw vegetables or crudités easily. Otherwise, vegetables can be steamed in a little ghee and served with mild spices.

Ideal: green leafy vegetables, crudités, artichokes, cauliflower, broccoli, potatoes,

sweet potatoes, okra, cucumbers, Brussels sprouts, peas, pumpkin, asparagus
Less recommended: onions, garlic, vegetables from the nightshade family such as eggplants and tomatoes, peppers, leek, radishes, horseradish

GRAIN
Grain is excellent for Pitta types.

Ideal: spelt, wheat, rice, oat, quinoa, kamut, quinoa, buckwheat, barley
Less recommended: corn, millet, rye

LEGUMES
Pitta constitutions obtain a lot of protein from legumes.

Ideal: mung dal, chana dal, brown lentils, beans
Less recommended: red lentils, chickpeas

FRUIT
Sweet, mature fruits with a cooling effect are particularly well tolerated by Pitta persons.

Ideal: apples, pears, grapes, melons, mangos, peaches, bananas, raspberries, papayas, pomegranates, figs, cherries, plums
Less recommended: sour oranges, grapefruit, apricots, strawberries, pineapples

DAIRY PRODUCTS
Dairy products that are not fermented are particularly appropriate for a Pitta diet.

Ideal: milk, whipped cream, cream cheese, ghee, butter, buttermilk
Less recommended: yogurt, kefir, hard cheese, cheese made from mold

FATS AND OILS
Most vegetable oils are warming; only ghee is cooling and coconut oil is neutral. The warming oils should only be consumed in small quantities. If possible, one should use cold-pressed fats and oils.

Ideal: ghee, coconut oil, olive oil, pumpkin seed oil, flaxseed oil, small amounts of sesame oil
Less recommended: canola oil, soybean oil

SWEETENERS
Sweeteners are essential for Pitta persons.

Ideal: dates, jaggery, raw brown sugar, rock sugar, sugar cane molasses

Not recommended: white sugar

SPICES
Spices that are not hot or sour can be used. Salt, more precisely rock salt, should only be used in small quantities.

Ideal: turmeric, coriander, cumin, cardamom, mint, bee balm, saffron, ajwain (caraway), ginger, dill, clove, sage, anise, basil, cinnamon
Less recommended: rosemary, marjoram, fenugreek, tamarind, nutmeg, paprika, garlic, sea salt, chili, mustard seeds, poppy seeds

NUTS AND SEEDS
Nuts and seeds are acceptable only in small quantities.

Ideal: coconuts, sunflower seeds, pumpkin seeds, almonds, flax seeds
Less recommended: sesame, cashew nuts, walnuts, hazelnuts, pine nuts
Not recommended: peanuts

Kapha-reduced diet

A Kapha diet should consist of warm, bitter, astringent, hot, light and dry dishes. Fasting is ideal for Kapha types as they feel much clearer and lighter during that process. One fasting day per week is perfect. Ginger tea with honey or hot water with Trikatu (3 spices: long peppers, ginger and black pepper) and honey can be consumed during the day. After sunset, one can have a light soup or a warm meal.

Kapha persons can easily skip breakfast and only have ginger or herbal tea. This should not be difficult for them as they are not very hungry in the early morning. Due to the omitted breakfast, Agni is stimulated, which makes lunch easily digestible. At 11:00 a.m. one can have fruit, for instance, a grated apple seasoned with lemon juice and honey or a freshly-squeezed juice. Crisp bread and rice cakes are also recommended.

Before lunch, one should have a pinch of Trikatu (spice blend made of ginger, long and black pepper) with honey. Lunch should be eaten as late in the day as possible, which is why dinner can be skipped or its amount can be greatly reduced. Since Kapha natures tend to gain weight easily, they should refrain from having dinner or only have little and light food in the evenings.

For lunch, it is important that the dishes are warm, hot and well-seasoned. A millet tofu stir fry with celery, leafy vegetables, a quinoa bell pepper chickpea stew with coriander chutney or a fresh lentil-vegetable curry with a bit of rice are ideal. A bit of crudités afterwards helps the digestion. One should absolutely skip dessert. One espresso without cream half an hour after the meal is acceptable.

Kapha natures tend to obesity, diabetes, edema, sinusitis and bronchitis and tend to sleep a lot.

Ideal food supplements are: Trikatu with honey, Triphala, Pippali (long pepper)

FOODS FOR KAPHA CONSTITUTIONS

VEGETABLES
Vegetables are particularly suitable for a Kapha diet, ideally with a bitter, hot and diuretic effect.

Ideal: root vegetables, broccoli, leafy vegetables, savoy cabbage, radishes, horseradish, green beans, Brussels sprouts, artichokes, asparagus, kohlrabi, green salad, endive, cress, almost any kind of fresh herbs, bell peppers, zucchini, eggplant
Less recommended: potatoes, tomatoes, cucumbers

GRAIN
Kapha persons need grain that is not heavy, moist or mucus dissolving. However, grain should only be consumed in small quantities.

Ideal: barley, quinoa, millet, buckwheat, corn, rice, kamut, rye, oat
Less recommended: wheat, spelt

LEGUMES
Due to their bitter taste, legumes are quite appropriate for a Kapha diet.

Ideal: all kinds of lentils, mung dal, beans

FRUIT
Fruit contains a lot of water, is light and, therefore, can be consumed by Kapha persons. Dried fruits are better than fresh ones, yet one needs to bear in mind their high amount of sugar. Astringent fruits are also suitable.

Ideal: apples, pears, citrus fruits, pineapples, papayas, pomegranates, dried fruits, raspberries, blueberries, currants, cherries, mango
Less recommended: melons, strawberries, bananas

DAIRY PRODUCTS
Dairy products should be avoided and only be occasionally consumed.

Ideal: buttermilk, whey, ghee (little), low-fat cheese, goat milk, goat milk cream cheese
Less recommended: cow's milk, yogurt, whipped cream, sour cream, hard cheese

FATS AND OILS
Fats and oils should only be consumed in small amounts.

Ideal: ghee, sesame oil, mustard oil, olive oil, coconut oil
Less recommended: sunflower oil, corn oil, any others

SWEETENERS
Sweeteners are to be cut out as much as possible.

Ideal: dates, honey (at least six months old), maple syrup, barley malt syrup, sugar cane molasses
Less recommended: any others

SPICES
Spices are rather important for a Kapha diet. The best type of salt to use would be rock salt.
Ideal: Any spices can be used with the exception of garlic

NUTS AND SEEDS
Nuts and seeds contain a lot of oil, are heavy and therefore not suitable for Kapha persons. Every now and then they can be consumed in small quantities.

Ideal: sunflower seeds, pumpkin seeds, almonds
Less recommended or little: sesame, walnuts, any others

Diet for mixed types

Nutritional advice for mixed constitutions is dependant on the currently dominant dosha and even more so on the weather season. Vatta/Pitta types with dominant Vata should stick to Vata tips in winter and Pitta tips in summer.

Person with Pitta/Kapha type should avoid Kapha-boosting and mucus like foods such as dairy, sugar and gluten cereals/grains in the spring. Similarly, in summer light food should be eaten (like salad, fruits and vegetables) to calm and soothe Pitta.

A Vata/Kapha person should follow a light diet with warm or hot dishes. He should only eat small amounts and exercise a lot. Depending on the dominating Dosha, one should either comply with dietary recommendations for a Vata- or a Kapha-reducing diet.

The good news is that winter is the season when the digestive fire "Agni" burns stronger due to the cold and then we can (all constitutions) digest more and heavier food. Most important is to listen to our body, strengthen digestive fire through a time regulated diet (fasting between meals) and eat organic, vegetarian food that we prepare ourselves with love.

The recipes in this cookbook are not divided into vata, pitta and kapha recipes. In moderation they are ideal for all the doshas and constitutions as they are made on sattva principle (no meat, eggs, fish, garlic, onion) and therefore optimal for all people.

AYURVEDIC EATING SUGGESTIONS OR HOW TO KEEP OJAS (VITAL POWER) LIVELY

- One should only eat when hungry and when the last meal is already digested
- There should be a time span of at least three to six hours between meals
- One should only eat sitting down
- Meals should be regular
- During a meal, one should not read or watch TV. Heated discussions should be avoided.
- Lunchtime or early afternoons are ideal for the main meal
- Do not eat after 6 p.m. (18:00)
- The stomach should only be half-full
- One can have a bit of juice, tea or water with meals, but drink only in small sips. Never drink right after a meal
- The main meal should contain all six flavors
- Do not have milk with meals. Drink separately, hot with spices. Exceptions are cereal, porridge, ripe mangos, unsulfured dried fruits, rice and nuts
- Do not have acidophilus milk products or fruit in the evening
- Do not cook or bake with honey as it produces Ama
- Ice-cold beverages should be avoided as they weaken digestion
- Always prepare the food fresh
- Use only high-quality organic products
- Make sure there is a relaxed and happy atmosphere while cooking
- A happy and conscious cook creates happy and satisfied eaters

Ayurvedic Morning Rituals and Detox

Rise before (or with) the sun between **5 a.m. and 7 a.m**. This is considered to be the most auspicious time of day, best time for meditation.

Oil pulling is a procedure that involves swishing oil in the mouth for oral and systemic health benefits. The sesame plant (Sesamum indicum) has been considered a gift of nature to mankind for its nutritional qualities and desirable health effects.

How to do it
1 tbsp of cold-pressed sesame oil
Take about 1 tablespoon of sesame oil and chew it, suck it through your teeth and swish around your mouth, for 10 and up to 15 minutes each morning after brushing and flossing your teeth (and using a tongue scrapper). Spit out and rinse with water, but don't rebrush. The slight oil coating is actually beneficial.

How to Tongue Scrape
Using a tongue scraper is easy: Simply place it toward the back of your tongue and drag it forward toward the tip of your tongue.

HOT WATER CURE

Bring one liter of water to a boil and let it simmer for ten minutes. Let the water sit for five minutes after boiling in order for the minerals in the water to settle.
Fill the water into a thermos flask and have a few sips from it every half hour. It is not important how much you drink from it, but how often.
Due to the boiling, the water's physical structure changes, i. e. the water becomes sweeter and softer. It bundles the metabolic waste (toxins) in the body and channels them out. Therefore, residues in the body will disappear.
A cure should last at least three to six weeks. Hot water does not substitute other drinks, such as teas, tap water and juices, but complements them. Hot water should be consumed as warm as possible. If you are a Pitta type, be more careful and use boiled, lukewarm water. This cleansing cure is suitable for almost any health problem. It is particularly efficient for reducing Ama, skin problems and helps with losing weight.

GINGER WATER

Boil few slices of fresh ginger (or 1-2 tsp. grated) in one liter of water for five minutes. Pour into a thermos flask and occasionally drink from it throughout the day.

Ginger water is particularly good for Kapha. It helps to digest, regulates the circulatory and the fat metabolism. Increased cholesterol can be reduced with ginger water. It can also regulate low blood pressure.

In order to lose weight, to purge and to fight colds, ginger water is especially appropriate. Pitta types should be careful as ginger water can produce additional warmth.

LEMON HONEY WATER

INGREDIENTS:

250 ml water
½ lemon, squeezed
1 tsp. honey

PREPARATION

Mix everything and drink instantly. The water should not be hot, but lukewarm as honey should not be heated over 45°C. This lemon honey water is ideal for losing weight, particularly for Kapha constitutions. Honey is considered as a fat killer, whereas lemon supports the liver and the pancreas.

credits to Greenmorning

GOLDEN MILK (CURCUMA LATTE)

The Golden Milk or milk with curcuma paste is an old proven Ayurveda recipe. Through the special preparation, the milk inhibits inflammation, acts as an anti-oxidant, inhibits cancer and strengthens the immune system, especially in winter. Curcuma can be easily absorbed in combination with fat and black pepper.

CURCUMA PASTE:

3 tablespoons of curcuma powder
¼ cup of water

PREPARATION:

Cook the paste in a small pot with a thick bottom, while stirring continuously, until it becomes a thick paste. Cool the paste and store in a glass jar with a screw-on lid in the refrigerator. The paste will remain fresh for 3-4 days.

credits to Greenmorning

1 CUP GOLDEN MILK:

1 teaspoon of curcuma paste
1 cup of organic milk or a plant-based milk (preferably almond, hemp or coconut milk)
2 pinches of ground black pepper
a few drops of coconut oil
1 teaspoon of maple syrup or raw organic sugar

PREPARATION:

Combine the ingredients in a small pot and cook it quickly, while stirring and enjoy it warm.

Rasayanas – Rejuvenation remedy

Foods that support firm body tissue, longevity, a strong mind, health, good looks, a healthy glow and increase resilience against illnesses.
With our daily diet, we can consume many of those rejuvenating foods.

- ghee (subtle and potent carrier of important substances) – the best fat, cholesterol-lowering, improves brain function, does not put a strain on the liver, bundles the metabolic waste (toxins) and channels them out of the body. Food prepared with ghee is a lot more digestible and tastier.
- carrots, mangos – vitamin A
- figs – iron
- dates – the best natural sweetener, brilliant source of energy bursting with vitamins and minerals
- grapes – phosphorous, calcium (helpful in reducing uterine fibroids and weight control)
- lemons, limes – good for the liver, very cleansing
- apples – rich in pectin, when boiled, very good for stomach, intestine and skin
- coconuts – calcium, vitamin B, cooling, good for hot flashes
- almonds – magnesium, high-quality protein, nourishes the nerves and brain, cancer-inhibiting, useful for alleviating menstrual pain
- pistachios – rich in iron, vitamin B
- cashew nuts – vitamin B, pantothenic acid (helps in the absorption with food)
- Brazil nuts – contains many body builders, comparable with egg protein, one nut covers the daily requirement of selenium
- fenugreek seeds – vitamin B, folate which is important during and after pregnancy, cleans the milk channels and stimulates the milk supply. Very good for liver, spleen, skin, hair and bones
- dill (greens and seeds) – helpful for alleviating PMS and menstrual cramps, for alleviating headaches and stomach aches as well as for relieving menopause afflictions and hot flashes
- nutmeg – soothing, relaxing
- cloves – blood-purifying, pain-relieving
- saffron – regulates menstruation, improves skin tone for a youthful glow
- asparagus – rich in iron
- cress – (greens and seeds) helpful in alleviating and preventing menopausal problems, contains a substance similar to estrogen
- mung dal – high-quality protein source
- legumes – best source of protein, helpful in alleviating and preventing menopausal problems,
balances the hormones
- honey and royal jelly
- Amalaki/Chyavanprash
- Shatavari – especially for women – Indian white asparagus (stimulates milk supply for breast-feeding mothers, cleanses the womb, useful in dealing with menopausal problems)
- Spirulina, wheatgrass, barley grass
- sugar cane molasses – rich in iron
- sesame, poppy seeds, hemp – strengthens teeth, skin, bones, high in calcium
- fresh herbs – such as parsley, dill, coriander, basil, thyme (contain many minerals and improve metabolism)
- Ashwagandha (Withania Somnifera) – especially for men – a powerful plant that can lower stress, strengthens men's sexual potency, improves fertility of both sexes, increases sperm count to up to 40 percent, an excellent nerve remedy

Wise spices

41

Wise Spices

AYURVEDIC MEDICINE CHEST
The most important Ayurvedic spices and how to use natural spice power

Spices play a main role in Ayurvedic cuisine. They enhance appetite, improve taste and neutralize some negative characteristics of certain food, for example, food which is heavy to digest, fried foods or foods with a tendency to produce gas. Spices can also be used in a therapeutic way.

AJWAIN (Wild celery/ lovage seeds)
Trachyspermum ammi

- inhibits flatulence
- bowel cleansing
- good for the respiratory tracts (as inhalation)
- It goes well good with potatoes, chowders, soups and flatbreads.

AMCHUR (Green Mango Powder)
Mangifera indica

- sour taste
- good by type 2 diabetes
- anti-inflammatory (especially
- helpful with tooth and gum problems, such as periodontitis)

Can be used for chutneys and hearty fillings, instead of citrus fruits.

ANISE SEEDS
Pimpinella anisum

- digestive
- against colic and flatulence
- good for the stomach

For chutneys, compote, stewed fruits, cakes and teas.

ASAFETIDA (Hing, Asant)
Ferula Assa-foetida

- prevents flatulence
- appetizing
- good instead of onion and garlic
  We use asafetida for all salty dishes instead of onions.

BAY LEAF (Tejpat)
Laurus nobilis

There are several ways to use bay leaves. If you are going to cook a bean or lentil dish, add a few leaves. It will enhance the taste and fragrance twice as much as the usual taste. I always use dried bay leafs.

BASIL
Ocimum basilicum

- balances all constitutions
- clears the mind
- anti-bacterial
- especially good for coughs and bronchitis
- strengthens the heart and immune system
- We do not use Tulsi (Ocimum sanctum) for cooking. Tulsi is a holy plant and should be carefully used as medicine in connection with mantras to increase the potency of the herb

BLACKSALT
(*Kala Namak, Sauvarchala Lavana*)

Blacksalt is a type of salt used together with rocksalt in ayurvedic cooking. It is known as Kala Namak salt and it is constituted mainly with sodium chloride with iron and sulphides. We use a redish-grey variety with a distinct "hard boiled egg" flavour. It is strong natural flavour enhancer. Food seasoned with blacksalt taste delicious.

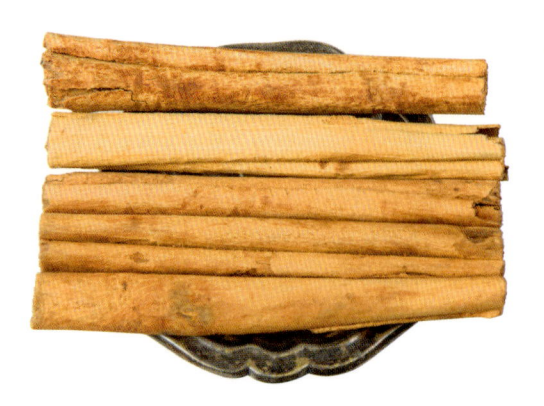

CARDAMOM, GREEN (Elaichi)
Elettaria cardamomum

- generally soothing
- when stirred into coffee, cardamom reduces the harmful effect of caffeine
- stimulates and strengthens the heart and supports brain function
- Main ingredient for sweet and spicy masalas. Rice cooked with cardamom is very aromatic.

CHILI (Mirch)
Capsicum annum

- it strengthens the digestive fire
- painkiller
- it boosts metabolism
- kills viruses, parasites and worms

CARAWAY SEEDS
Carum carvi

In traditional European cuisine, caraway seeds are one of the dominant spices featuring in many savory dishes. Strongly aromatic, caraway is a member of the parsley or Umbelliferae family; a large family of herbs that also includes commonly-known herbs and spices such as anise, fennel, cumin, etc.

CINNAMON (Dalchini)
Cinnamomum verum,
Cinnamom zeylanicum

- warming
- sweetening, stimulates circulation
- regulates blood sugar (therefore good for people with diabetes)

The bark of tree is used as a spice. The bark of new trees is slippery and oily

whereas the bark of old trees is dry and brown.
The bark of cinnamon is widely used to provide an aromatic flavour to dishes like biryanis, curries, beans, lentils, etc.
It is also used in many dessert recipes like pies, candy, patties, coffee, etc.
Cinnamon is a basic ingredient in spicy chai teas and even milk tea.
It is a popular flavouring ingredient in alcoholic beverages.
Taking cinnamon with honey and water is helpful when losing weight and also to curb many disorders.

CLOVES (Lavang)
Syzygium aromaticum

- bud-type flowers which are dried
- anti-inflammatory, anti-fungal
- painkiller
- warming
- blood-purifying
- induces perspiration

Cloves are widely used in Asian, African and Middle-East cuisines in the cooking of curries, gravy, sauces and marinades. Important ingredient for different masalas such as curry or garam masala.

CORIANDER / CILANTRO (Dhania)
Coriandrum sativum

- Allergen-fighter
- The leaves and tender stems of the plant are used as a fresh herb (referred to as cilantro) and the seeds, whole or ground, as a dry spice (coriander).
- Allergic reactions result from improper digestion and an accumulation of ama (toxins) in the physiology, which weakens the immune system and distorts the body's normal response mechanisms. Cilantro and coriander, by enhancing digestion, work to alleviate the root cause of allergic reactions.
- Coriander is cooling, pain-relieving, soothing, anti-inflammatory, helps with skin diseases, can channel heavy metals, useful for urinary tract problems
- The leaves of coriander are widely used as a garnishing ingredient in curries, soups, fast foods and gravy. The seeds are my favourite spice for all hearty dishes.

CURCUMA/ TURMERIC (Haldi)
Curcuma longa

- blood-purifying
- antiseptic, can stop bleeding
- especially good for digestion of protein
- daily prevention against cancer
- supports liver and gall bladder function
- has an anti-allergic properties
- antithrombotic effect (inhibits blood clotting)
- in combination with black pepper, curcuma is anti-inflammatory
- The turmeric root belongs to the ginger or Zingiberaseae family of root herbs. Just a few grams of turmeric per day either in the form of powder, crushed root or fresh root can provide enough nutrients to prevent anemia, neuritis, memory disorders and offer protection against cancers, infectious diseases, high blood pressure and strokes. Use fresh root (grated) or high-quality organic powder in everyday cooking for all salty dishes.

CURRY LEAVES (Kadi Patta)
Bergera coenigii

- rich source of iron and folic acid
- highly aromatic when fresh
- important ingredient in South India kitchens
- very similar to bay leaf but curry leaves are to be eaten whole. Use fresh leaves if you can; they are generally available in Asian stores.

CUMIN (Jeera)
Cuminum cyminum

- balancing for all three doshas
- very effective in inhibiting flatulence, digestive
- Cumin is strongly aromatic. The flavor and aroma emerge best if they have been dry roasted or added to hot ghee. Use for raitas, savories, legumes and cabbage dishes.

FENUGREEK (Methi)
Trigonela foenum-graecum semen

- warming
- helps in weight reduction
- enhances hair growth
- effective remedy for liver problems and lack of power
- the best ayurvedic medicine for diabetes
- stimulates breast milk supply in combination with cane sugar
- decreases blood sugar and cholesterol
- aphrodisiac
- carrier of bitter taste

Used for all curries and Indian food.

FENNEL (Saunf)
Foeniculum vulgare semen

- cooling
- sweet
- helps against stomach and intestinal colic
- very good for the spleen
- It goes nicely with dal dishes or fried legumes like falafel

GINGER (Adrak)
Zingiber officinale

- "universal medicine", warming, prevents an accumulation of metabolic waste, helps alleviate flatulence and nausea, eases acute diarrhea in combination with yogurt, helps relieve a sore throat and cough
- everyone should eat fresh ginger just before lunch and dinner to enhance digestion

- improves assimilation and transportation of nutrients to targeted body tissues
- clears the microcirculatory channels of the body
- In addition to the above situations, ginger is an excellent spice that can be used daily.
- Modern science, by way of worldwide research, ratifies its effectiveness in preventing motion or airsickness, improving digestion and for its analgesic effect on the joints, particularly in early stages of rheumatoid arthritis.
- If you can eat raw ginger, a good way to take it is to dip two or three thin slices of ginger in a little salt and lime juice and eat them before the main meal.
- The best way to cook with ginger is to sauté some grated ginger in a teaspoon of ghee before adding all other ingredients or add some grated ginger to warm milk (add sweetener if you like), desserts or other dishes.

MARJORAM
Origanum majorana

Marjoram is a member of Labiatae family, in the genus, Origanum. It has delicate sweet flavour and is subtly pungent. Fresh or dried marjoram can be used as a flavoring in the preparation of salad dressings, soups, stews and patties (savoury dishes).
It is an excellent source of iron and vitamin K.

MINT (Pudina)
Mentha piperata, Mentha spicata, Mentha arvensis

Mint is one of the oldest and most popular herbs grown around the world. There are many different varieties of mint, each having its own subtle flavour and aroma. This herb is used in a range of dishes from stuffing to fruit salads or chutneys. Peppermint oil has analgesic, local anesthetic and counter-irritant properties. It has been used in the preparation of topical muscle relaxants and analgesics. It is also useful in the treatment of respiratory disorders, cough, nausea and headache. If possible, always use fresh leaves of peppermint or spearmint.

NIGELLA (black cumin seeds, Kalonji)
Nigella sativa

- cleanses blood
- kills many parasites and worms
- good for the stomach and digestion
- helps with all skin disease

In the Arabian world, it is known as "black gold". The seeds of the Nigella sativa are used for flavoring and to improve digestion. Best in stews, potatoes, flatbreads, pumpkin or sweet potato dishes.

NUTMEG (Jaiphal)
Myristica fragrans

- use only a pinch (otherwise it can be toxic)
- an excellent nerve tonic that it is consumed in very small quantities (about one pinch)
- higher doses are poisonous
- useful for the treatment of sleep disorder
- improves the absorption of nutrients in the small intestine

As a naturally warming spice, this herb is used in Ayurvedic cooking along with other spices like bay leaves, black pepper and cinnamon. Ayurvedic texts suggest the use of a pinch of nutmeg powder in warm milk before going to bed to calm the nerves, stimulate the system and promote peaceful sleep.

OREGANO
Origanum vulgare

- Oregano oil and leaves are both strong herbal antibacterial agents due to the high thymol content.
- The dried leaves are used in hot compresses to treat painful swellings and rheumatism.
- Oregano tea is a strong sedative and is traditionally used to treat colds, bronchitis, asthma, fevers and painful menstruation because of its antiseptic action.

Use for all Mediterranean dishes, patties, hearty soups and stews.

PARSLEY (Ajmood)
Petroselinum crispum

The two major groups of parsley used as herbs are curly leaf or flat leaf. It can be used as a garnish and flavoring agent. Parsley is strong diuretic herb with high content of iron.

PEPPER, LONG (Pippali)
Piper Longum

Long Pepper is a very unique spice known as a "tridoshic" herb, as it is suitable for all body-types. Taste is pungent and sweet. It has rejuvenative qualities useful in indigestion, asthma, cough, blood-cleansing etc. but it is also a very good aphrodisiac and anti aging spice.

PEPPER, BLACK (Kali Mirch)
Piper Nigrum

Useful in the treatment of respiratory disorders and weak digestion.
Every dish can benefit from a pinch of black pepper. Black pepper enhances bioavailability of Turmeric.

ROCKSALT, UNREFINED (Saindhava Lavana),
Himalayan pink salt

Saindhava lavana or rock salt is considered best among all salts. We use only unrefined natural rocksalt.

ROSEMARY
Rosmarinus officinalis

Ayurvedic medicine celebrates rosemary oil as one of the standard inhalations for treating respiratory disorders, sinusitis and gall bladder problems.
Use for casserole and oven dishes.

SAGE
Salvia officinalis

It helps to improve the condition of the brain, nerves, eyes and glands. It has a strong aroma and it has a bitter and astringent taste. It is known to quicken the senses and memory and it regulates excessive sweating. If possible, use fresh leaves as a spice. Dried ones can be used for tea.
If you cook polenta from corn semolina or a pasta dish, use a lot of sage.

SAFFRON (Kesar)
Crocus sativus

Saffron is a royal spice. In Ayurveda, saffron is considered tridoshic — balancing for all doshas. It helps in the assimilation of nutrients. The cost of saffron production is very high and saffron is the world's most expensive spice (it takes 70,000 flowers to produce a half kilo of saffron). Persian (or Iranian) saffron is a natural spice and we call it Red Gold. It is known globally for its incomparable quality, fascinating fragrance, pleasant flavor and superb coloring strength. Always grind the saffron threads in a stone mortar and add some hot water. You will get the saffron essence which you can use for further cooking like rice, puddings, cakes, etc.

- cooling
- aphrodisiac
- regulating effect on menstruation
- suggested to improve poor sperm production

STAR ANISE
Illicium verum

This beautiful spice is the star-shaped fruit of the small evergreen tree. It has a very spicy, anise-like flavor. It is an ingredient in the Chinese five-spice powder. Small amounts are used, as the spice is powerful in flavour. Star anise has carminative, digestive, stimulant and diuretic properties. Use for chutneys or poached fruits.

TAMARIND (Imli)
Tamarindus indica

Tamarind is the pulp extracted from the brown pods of the tamarind tree. The pulp is used as a flavouring for its sweet, sour, fruity aroma and taste. Tamarind is high in acid, sugar and B vitamins. It is considered a mild laxative and digestive. It contains pectin which is used in the manufacturing process of commercially-produced jams, so it is a natural ingredient in many jams, jellies, fruit drinks and Worcestershire sauce. Usually, it is the juice or paste that is used as a souring agent for lentil dishes, curries and chutneys

THYME
Thymus vulgaris

Thyme herb is packed with numerous health-benefiting phyto-nutrients (plant-derived compounds) and minerals and vitamins that are essential for overall wellness. Thyme herb contains thymol, one of the important essential oils.
Thymol has been found scientifically to have antiseptic and anti-fungal characteristics. Thyme is used in the preparation of seasonings, soups, sauces and pasta.

VANILLA
Vanilla planifolia

Vanilla beans are pleasantly fragrant fruit pods obtained from the tropical climbing orchid, V. planifolia. They are one of the expensive spices used especially as a flavoring agent in wide variety of sweet drinks and confectionaries.

Ideal combination and preparation of dishes

Components of a complete menu:
- grain
- vegetables
- protein (legume such as beans or lentils, nuts, natural dairy products, seeds) the rest consists of liquid and fats

For lunch, any type of grain with seasonal vegetables and a protein source, such as lentils, dairy products or nuts, should be consumed every day. Vegetarians should mix lentils with carbohydrates as this helps our body to ingest the amino acids better.

One should not drink a lot with food. Always have lukewarm or hot drinks and never consume ice-cold beverages.

All six flavours should be contained in one lunch. Only in that way can one achieve a feeling of satiety that lasts.

Ahimsa Milk (raw or pasteurized, in no case homogenized or UHT milk) should ideally always be consumed hot with spices and a bit of ghee. Do not mix with other food apart from wheat, rice, nuts, dried fruits (unsulfured), Chyavanprash, mangos, cane sugar or honey.

Milk should by no means be mixed with salt, garlic, vegetables, meat or seafood as this can cause digestive disorders and metabolic waste.

A large spoonful of yogurt or a highly-blended lassi (only in summer) along with lunch improves digestion and nutrient intake.

One does not need to cook four to six different dishes to have an ideal menu. What is most important is that one menu contains all the important nutrients. If you know where to find which nutrient, it is easy to compile an appropriate menu.

The following list is supposed to support you in doing so:
- protein: dairy products, all legumes and lentils, nuts, seeds
- carbohydrates: all grains, potatoes, sweet potatoes, pumpkin
- vitamins, minerals, fiber and trace elements: vegetables, fruit, herbs, spices
- fats: ghee, oil, dairy products, nuts, kernels

Some examples of dishes that contain all the nutrients and can be prepared quickly and easily:

- mung dal soup with vegetables and pasta
- small chickpea patties with salad
- vegetable spelt semolina stew with nuts
- small millet carrot loafs with salad and yogurt coconut raita
- Ayurvedic lasagna with vegetables and cheese
- potato eggplant lentil casserole
- kitchari (rice, dal and vegetable stew)
- yellow lentils with potatoes
- spicy roasted potato nut stew
- glazed wok vegetables with tofu and rice
- white bean celery tomato soup with bread
- hummus (chickpea spread) with bread and crudités
- sesame rice with green beans, carrots and tofu
- paneer cheese with chard and potatoes

If certain foods do not agree with our disposition, we can reduce their negative effect with the opposing characteristics of spices. A heavy dish, such as heavy grain, can be lightened with ginger, cloves or cardamom.

Flatulent types of lentils and vegetables, such as cabbage and brown lentils, can be neutralized with flatulent-inhibiting spices such as cumin, ajwain and coriander.

Dry foods, such as dried fruits, cereal flakes and beans, can be made more digestible by soaking.

Mucous foods, such as milk, should be a heated up and lightened with warming spices (cinnamon, cloves, turmeric, anise, ginger).

Yogurt should always be consumed blended as a beverage and never in the evening.

Have cheese only in small quantities and in combination with hot spices such as black pepper, red paprika, basil and turmeric.

Raw fruits should be consumed separately or before a meal.

Measurements

HOW TO USE RECIPES IN THIS BOOK

I am using very simple measuring in this book. There are some differences between American, English and Australian measurements in form of teaspoon, tablespoon and cups:

teaspoon - tsp. - 5 ml
(approximately all teaspoons in all three countries are the same)
tablespoon - tbsp. - American 14,2 ml, British 17,7 ml and Australian 20 ml
(although the slight difference does not really matter for the recipe to be successful)
cup - c. - 250 ml

Measurements of weight have been given in grams.
Measurements of temperature are in Celsius and then in Fahrenheit.
Measurements of length are given in centimetres.

Masalas – spice mix powder

There are countless masalas that match with various dishes. They are the flavor carriers of Ayurvedic dishes. Masalas can be prepared in advance and be spread on finished dishes just like curry powder or garam masala.

However, depending on the dish, one should ideally use fresh spice mixes every day.

Spices are either to be roasted in a frying pan with hot ghee or dry without fat (these are mostly spices that are made to keep in stock, so they are more durable).

For daily use, they can be roasted in hot fat (1 – 2 tbsp.). Not every spice needs an equal amount of time when roasting, which is why the preparation of masala is a special skill and requires knowledge of various types and compositions of spices. This type of preparation – browning the spices in order to set the aromas and flavors free – is unique to Ayurveda and may differ from country to country.

Either whole or crushed seeds or finely-ground spices are used. Whole seeds take longer when roasting, which is why you put them into the frying pan first, then add seeds crushed in a mortar and finally add spice powder. Fresh ginger is added at the end and also needs to be roasted for a few seconds. That is how it loses its sharpness and becomes sweet and spicy.

Masalas can be prepared at the beginning of cooking a meal by heating ghee in a sauce pan, adding the spices, roasting, then adding vegetables and finally some water. Alternatively, one can, for example, finish boiling a lentil dish only in water and roast the spices in a small sauce or frying pan. Add the masala at the end. Lentil dishes are particularly well-suited for this technique.

CURRY POWDER

INGREDIENTS:

2 tbs. fennel seeds
2 tbs. cumin seeds
10 pc. cloves
1 tbs. black mustard seeds
1 tsp. black peppercorns
1 tbs. fenugreek seeds
4 tbs. curcuma powder

PREPARATION:

Heat a heavy frying pan and add cumin seeds. Roast and stir until the nutty aroma comes out (approximately 1-2 minutes). Add all other spices apart from curcuma. Roast and stir until spices have acquired a dark-brown color and developed a nice, nutty aroma (ca. 2-3 minutes).
Leave to cool and grind as finely as possible in a coffee grinder. Mix with curcuma and store in a closed jar.
This spice blend is ready to use and should not be roasted a second time, but added to a finished dish.

GARAM MASALA

INGREDIENTS:

2 tbsp. cumin seeds
2 cinnamon sticks
(break several times)
10 pc. cloves
4 tbsp. coriander seeds
1 tsp. black peppercorns
10 pc. green cardamom capsules

PREPARATION:

Roast all spices in a frying pan continuously tossing until they become dark-brown and develop a fresh roasted aromas. Usually, that is the case after 2 or 3 minutes. Leave it to cool and grind in a coffee grinder as finely as possible. Store in a tightly-closed jar.

This spice blend is ready to use and should not be roasted a second time, but added to a finished dish.

SAMBAR MASALA

INGREDIENTS:

1/2 cup (120 ml) coriander seeds
1 tbsp. fenugreek seeds
1 tbsp. cumin seeds
1 tbsp. black peppercorns
2 pc. dried red chili peppers
1 tbsp. urad dal
1 tbsp. chana dal
2 tbsp. turmeric powder

PREPARATION:

Heat a heavy frying pan and add the two dals. Roast for 3-5 minutes. Set aside in one pot. Toast the remaining ingredients apart from turmeric powder. It takes 2-3 minutes. Set aside, leave to cool, mix with dal and grind as finely as possible in a coffee grinder. At the end, mix with curcuma and store in a closed jar.
This spice blend is ready to use and should not be roasted a second time, but added to a finished dish.

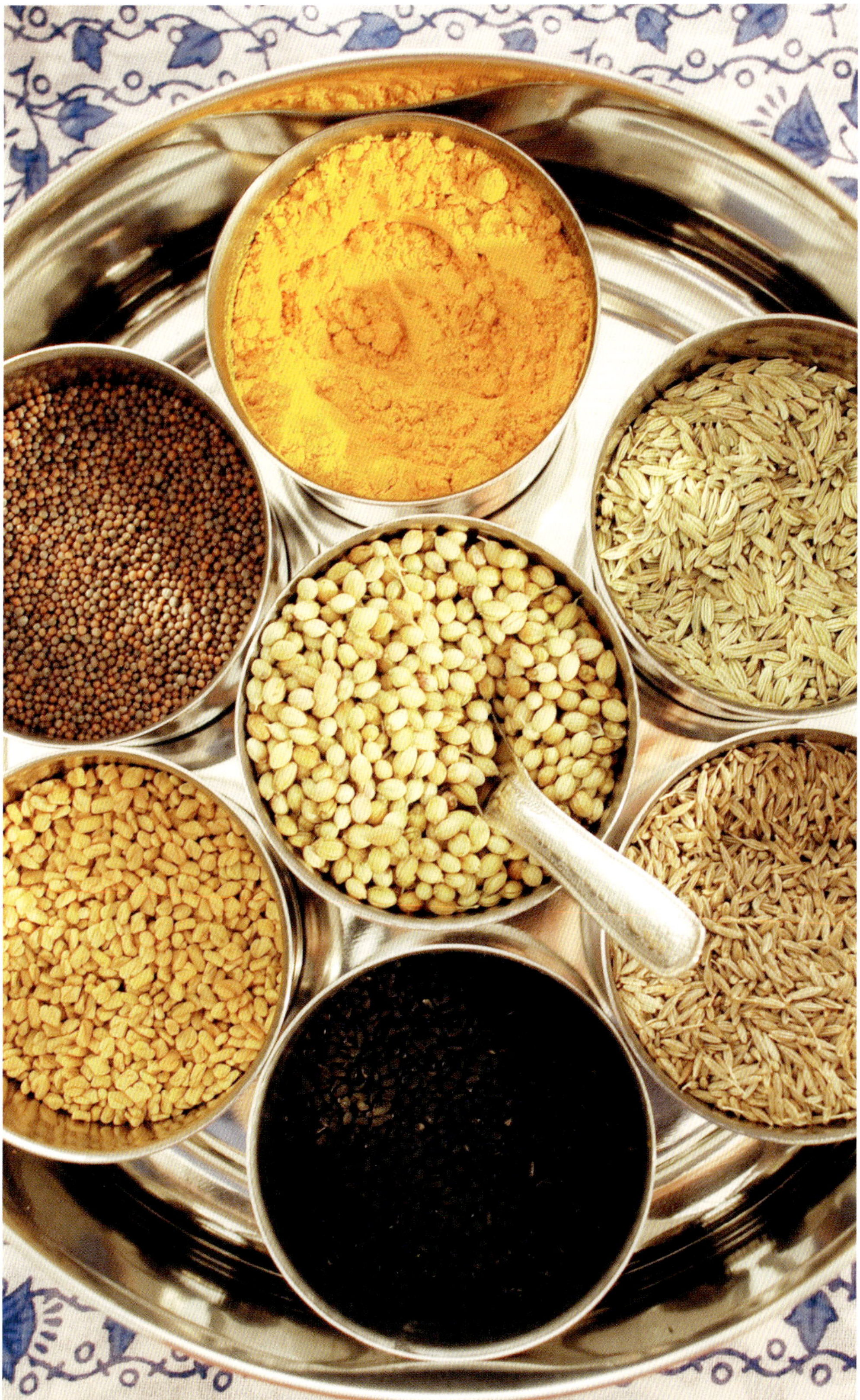

Introduction to recipes and yogic way of cooking

The original Ayurveda cuisine is Yogic and lacto-vegetarian. That means that it is intended for people who are developing mentally and spiritually. Therefore, the recipes in this cookbook contain no onions or garlic as they dull the mind and irritate the senses. There is a variety of spices, which, if combined and used cleverly, substitute bulbous plants in dishes rather well.

Cooking according to Ayurveda is a spiritual ritual through which the divine is honored. The creator provides us with the fruit of nature and we thank him before we consume the food. Consequently, one should cook attentively and with devotion, without tasting the food while cooking.

Only after having said a prayer or a mantra and when the dishes are ready served on the table, can we enjoy the food. In that way, we have enough strength to digest properly and feed our body, mind & soul.

Having such a diet can have an immensely positive influence, even a healing effect and a positive impact on our thoughts since mind and intelligence are nourished by the food's finest essence. Furthermore, we know that almost all illnesses are evoked psychosomatically. Hippocrates said:

"Let food be thy medicine and medicine be thy food."

61

Breakfast

1.

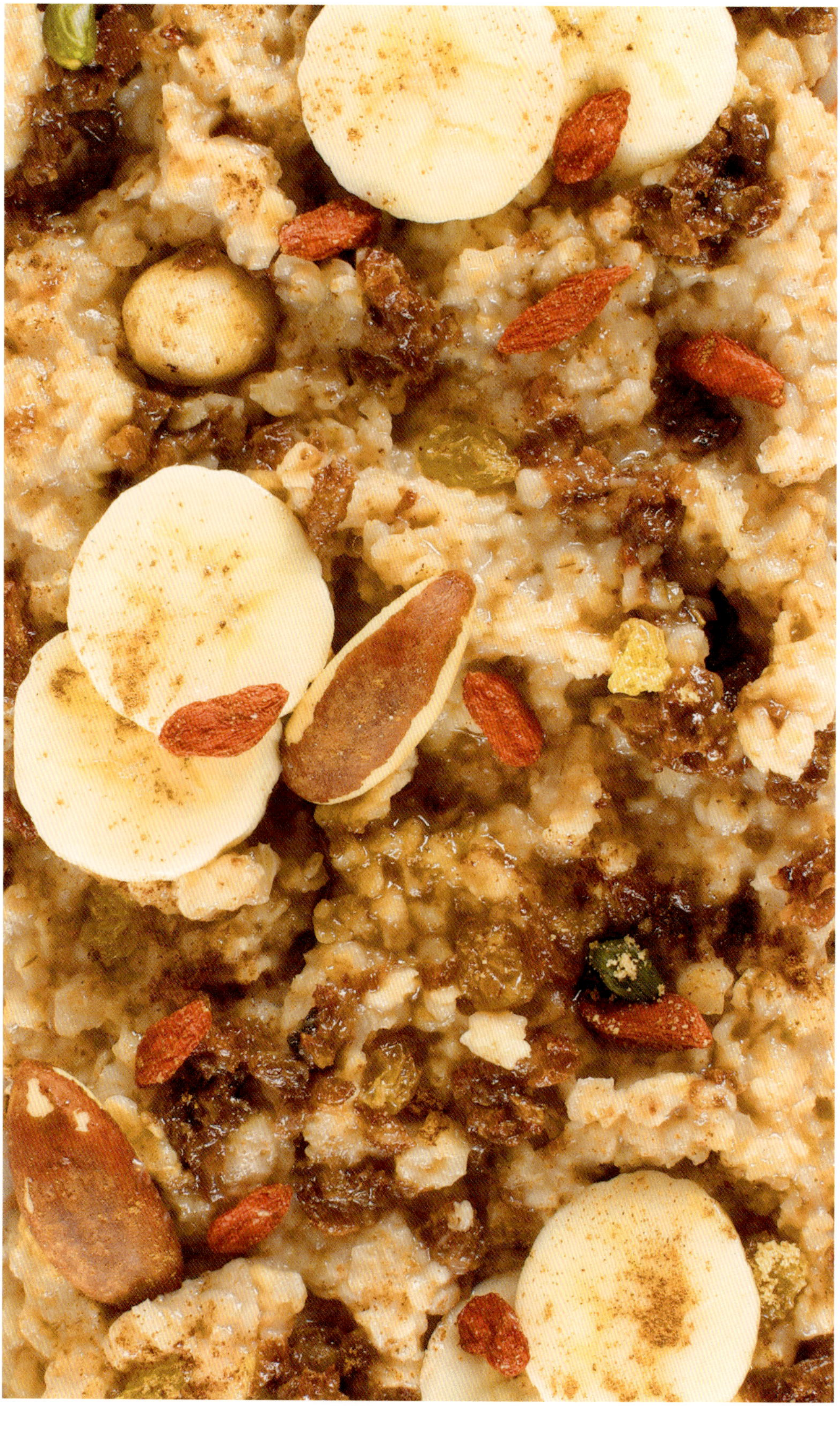

AYURVEDA CLASSICS
Fresh grain porridge for breakfast

Breakfast should be warm and nourishing. Note: for Vata and Pitta, a little more ghee and heavy grain types, such as wheat, spelt and oats, are used. For Kapha, lighter grain and pseudo cereal, such as millet and barley, are used. Any variety of rice is good, depending on the quantity.

Porridge is purging, soothing and regulates digestion at the same time. It nourishes and renews all seven body tissues, donates energy and strengthens the vital force, in Ayurveda called "Ojas."

Breakfast porridge is always prepared with water as it ought to be easily digestible. There is an exception if the porridge is supposed to rejuvenate or boost and build new tissues. In that case, it is called "Rasayana" and is best for Vata and Pitta types. These types of porridge are particularly recommended after a "Panca Karma cure" (cleansing therapy) and gradually build up new tissue. In that case, one prepares semolina or any cereal porridge with milk and uses dried, unsulfured fruits instead of fresh ones.

CEREAL PORRIDGE
1 people

INGREDIENTS:

70 ml whole grain cereal flakes – spelt, wheat, barley, millet, oat or rice
1 apple – peeled and chopped into small pieces
½ tsp. ghee / virgin coconut oil
1 tbsp. raw cane sugar, maple syrup or barley malt syrup
1 tbsp. raisins, dates or other dried fruits (optional)

Possible spices:
cinnamon, clove powder, ginger, cardamom powder, saffron, anise or shredded coconut – but not all at once

about 350 ml water or as required to get sticky pudding

PREPARATION:

Roast pieces of apple in a bit of ghee, add spices and pour in water. Bring the mixture to a boil, add flakes and let it boil for about 5-10 minutes until you have a thick mash. Finally, stir in the sugar.

Instead of flakes, whole grain semolina can also be used. Make sure you only use organic grain.

SHREDDED CEREAL PORRIDGE
1 people

INGREDIENTS:

70 ml shredded grain
300 ml water
1 tbsp. raisins or other dried fruits such as apricots, dates or figs
1 tbsp. raw cane sugar, maple syrup or barley malt syrup
½ tsp. ghee / virgin coconut oil
1 pinch of cinnamon or cardamom powder
1 apple, pear or other fruits, chopped into small pieces

One can use any kind of grain. The most appropriate ones are barley, kamut (khorasan), spelt, oat, millet and rice. The grain should be ground roughly to a texture a bit rougher than semolina.

PREPARATION:

Bring water to a boil. Add grain gradually and simultaneously stir with a whisk in order to avoid lumps. Add fruits and let it simmer slowly for about 5 minutes. Finally, add ghee, sugar and spices.

One can steam the fruits separately or serve it with the porridge as a purée.

NOTE: In this book, there are only two porridge recipes because there are countless variations of these; it only depends on which type of grain, spices, fruit or water/milk you use. Beautiful porridge can be created with seasonal berries, bananas, peaches or cherries. Use some chopped almonds or walnuts for protein. Also, ground flaxseeds can be added for additional digestive support. Try to add some coconut milk at the end - it will make the porridge very creamy and light. And ... do not forget cardamom!

BROCCOLI AND ALMOND SPREAD
6-8 people

INGREDIENTS:

1 head of broccoli
100 g almonds, peeled
1 tbsp. maple syrup
1 tsp. mustard (paste)
1 lemon, squeezed
1 tsp. black salt (kala namak)
½ tsp. black pepper
3-4 tbsp. virgin sunflower oil
1-2 tbsp. fresh herbs - cilantro or parsley

PREPARATION:

Wash the broccoli and cut into large pieces. Steam the broccoli about 5 minutes, until it is al dente. Grind the almonds finely in a coffee grinder, nut grater, or food processor. Using a food processor, mix together the ground almonds, mustard, lemonjuice, salt, oil, pepper, maple syrup, herbs and water until creamy.

Add in broccoli pieces and mix until creamy. If necessary, you can use a hand mixer to purée it more. Refrigerate.

HUMMUS CHICKPEA SESAME SPREAD
6-8 people

INGREDIENTS:

200 g chickpeas, soaked overnight
2 tbsp. sesame butter (tahini)
1 lemon, squeezed
5-6 tbsp. olive oil
1 tsp. salt
½ tsp. black pepper
cumin or caraway powder for garnishing

PREPARATION:

Soak the chickpeas overnight. Cook at least 2 hours with plenty of water. Drain well and rinse in cold water.

Mix the chickpeas with the other ingredients in a food processor to a smooth paste. The paste should be uniform without large chickpea pieces. If necessary, you can add 2-3 tbsp. of water while processing.

SMOKY TOFU & SUNFLOWER SEED SPREAD
4-6 people

INGREDIENTS:

100 ml (⅓ cup) sunflower seeds, finely ground
100 g smoked tofu, mashed in a food processor
½ tsp. black pepper
½ tsp. black salt (kala namak)
⅓ tsp. cayenne powder
1 tsp. mustard (paste)
100 ml of water or as required

PREPARATION:

Place all ingredients in a food processor and blend until thick & smooth.
   Finished!

PANEER CURRY HERB SPREAD
4-6 people

INGREDIENTS:

200 g paneer - homemade cheese or ricotta (see page 94)
1 tsp. curry powder
1 tbsp. fresh herbs, mixed - dill, marjoram or parsley
1 tbsp. melted butter
1 tbsp. sour cream
⅓ tsp. black pepper
½ tsp. black salt (kala namak)

PREPARATION:

Mix all ingredients quickly in a food processor to make a paste. Refrigerate.
   Done.

AVOCADO-PUMPKIN SEED AND BASIL SPREAD
4-6 people

INGREDIENTS:

50 g pumpkin seeds, finely ground (optional)
1 avocado
10 fresh basil leaves, cut into strips
1 pinch asafetida
½ tsp. black salt
½ tsp. black pepper
½ lemon, squeezed

PREPARATION:

Cut the avocado cut in half, remove core and peel. Cut into pieces.

Add all the ingredients into a food processor and grind to a paste. Refrigerate and consume the same day.

BROWN OR GREEN LENTIL TAHINI SPREAD
6-8 people

INGREDIENTS:

200 g brown or green lentils
(soaked for 1-2 hours)
4 tbsp. olive oil
1 tbsp. tahini (sesame butter)
1 tbsp. breadcrumbs
1 tsp. salt
½ tsp. black pepper
2 tbsp. parsley, finely chopped
2 pinches asafetida
½ tsp. garam masala
1 lemon, squeezed
½ tsp. sweet paprika powder
½ tsp. ground cumin
1 pinch of chili powder

PREPARATION:

Wash lentils and place in a pot with ½ l of water. Bring to a boil. Simmer for 30 minutes and stir occasionally. After 30 minutes, lentils should be cooked but not falling apart. If they are still hard, simmer for another 5-10 minutes. Rinse the lentils in cold water and drain well.

Mix all the ingredients in a food processor to a smooth paste. Refrigerate.

Soups

2.

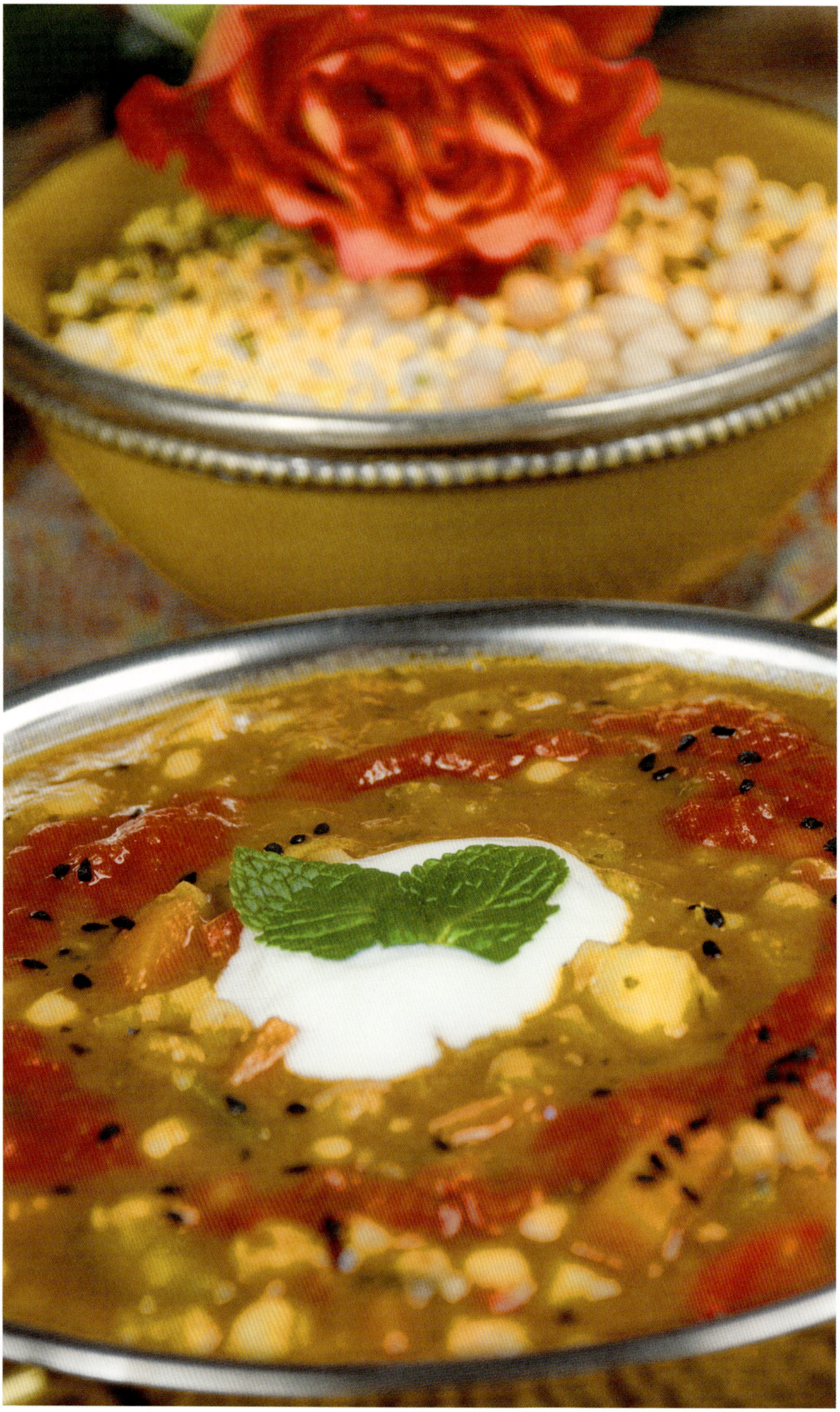

SOUPS
For the soul

Soups are a gift for the body and soul, regardless of whether they are clear or creamy or served with side dishes. They can be eaten as an appetizer or for lunch or dinner.
 Soups provide moisture, warmth, and they strengthen and tone up the intestines and nervous system. Creamy soups are best in the winter and are excellent for balancing Vata types. For Pitta types, hearty soups with garnishes or additional ingredients are recommended. Clear, light broths with many herbs are ideal for Kaphas.

Soups are excellent for fasting because they maintain the body heat better than conventional fasting (juice fasting, for example). Waste products are burned away and excreted. Gastric and intestinal mucous membranes are regenerated in a gentle way and the digestion is restored.

The best soup for detoxing is a thin kitchari soup from husked mung dal and rice.

RED LENTIL CAULIFLOWER SOUP
2-4 people

INGREDIENTS:

Ingredients:
½ cup (100 g) red lentils
½ head of cauliflower
2 carrots or turnips
2 potatoes
½ green or red bell pepper
1 tsp. grated fresh ginger
1 pinch asafetida
½ tsp. turmeric
½ tsp. coriander powder
½ tsp. cumin powder
½ lime, squeezed
1 tsp. salt
1-2 tsp. ghee or virgin coconut fat
1 tbsp. fresh coriander, finely chopped
3 cups (750 ml) water

PREPARATION:

Wash and boil red lentils. Skim off the foam. Wash the vegetables and cut into small pieces. Add carrots and potatoes and simmer for 10 minutes. Add the cauliflower and red pepper and cook for another 10 minutes. In a separate pot, heat the ghee and fry the spices. Add the finished masala to the vegetable soup.

Finally, add salt, fresh coriander and lime juice. Reheat and serve.

ROOT VEGETABLES CREAM SOUP
2 people

INGREDIENTS:

¼ celeriac
1-2 carrots
2 potatoes
small piece of leek
(10 cm/1-2 inches)
2 tbsp. coconut milk
2 tbsp. olive oil
½ tsp. black salt (or plain rock salt)
½ tsp. of black pepper
Spice mix:
1 pinch asafetida
½ tsp. turmeric
½ tsp. coriander powder
Fresh herbs (parsley, dill, or coriander)

PREPARATION:

Wash and cut the vegetables into big pieces. Heat up the olive oil and sauté the vegetables for one minute. Add all the spices except the fresh herbs, salt & pepper and sauté another 30 seconds. Add about 2 cups (500 ml) water and cook for about 25 minutes.

Add the coconut milk, fresh herbs, salt and pepper. Purée to a fine consistency with a hand blender or food processor.

MUNG DAL BARLEY VEGETABLE SOUP
2-4 people

INGREDIENTS:

100 g mung dal
1 fennel
1 carrot
3 mangold leaves (chard) (optional)
2 tbsp. barley (soaked for 1 hour or overnight)
½ tsp. cumin powder
½ tsp. coriander powder
½ tsp. fenugreek powder
1 pinch asafetida
1 tsp. turmeric
1 tsp. salt
1 tsp. fresh ginger (grated)
½ lemon, squeezed
¾ l of water
1-2 tsp. ghee or virgin coconut fat

PREPARATION:

Rinse the mung dal and barley and boil in 3 cups (750 ml) of water. Skim off the foam and simmer about 10 minutes. Dice the carrots and fennel and add to the soup. Simmer another 15-20 minutes. Wash the mangold (chard) well, cut into small pieces and add. In a separate small saucepan, heat the ghee, and then add the spices and fresh ginger and fry. Add the masala to the dal-barley-vegetable mixture.

Finally, season to taste with salt and lemon juice.

TIP:

This soup is ideal for fasting, detoxing and purifying. It is especially good for Kapha types.

QUINOA VEGETABLE SOUP
2-4 people

INGREDIENTS:

2 carrots
¼ celeriac
½ cup green beans or green peas
½ kohlrabi
2-3 tbsp. quinoa grains
¼ tsp. thyme
½ tsp. turmeric
1 pinch asafetida
½ tsp. coriander powder
½ tsp. lovage or other soup herbs
2 tbsp. olive oil
1 pinch black pepper
1 tsp. black salt
3 cups (750 ml) water
2 tomatoes, finely chopped

PREPARATION:

Wash the vegetables and cut into small pieces. Rinse quinoa well with warm water. Heat the olive oil in a pot, add the spices, and fry briefly. Add the chopped vegetables (except tomatoes) and fry over low heat for another 2 minutes. Now pour the water in, add the quinoa and simmer for about 20 minutes. Add the tomatoes and simmer another 5 minutes. Finally, add salt and fresh herbs.

RED BEET AND POTATO DILL SOUP
2-4 people

INGREDIENTS:

2 beets, peeled and sliced
2 potatoes, peeled and sliced
⅓ tsp. asafetida
½ tsp. turmeric
2 bay leaves
½ tsp. coriander powder
1 tsp. salad herbs or lovage, dry (optional)
1 tbsp. fresh dill, finely chopped
½ lemon or lime
1 tsp. black salt (kala namak)
½ tsp. ground black pepper
3 cups (¾ l) water
2 tbsp Tahini sesame paste
(or add some oat flakes)
1-2 tsp. ghee or virgin coconut oil

PREPARATION:

Heat the ghee in a pan, fry beets and all the spices (except salt). Pour in 1 l of water, cover, and simmer for about 25 minutes. Add the potatoes and simmer for another 20 minutes. Remove the bay leaf, add salt, lemon juice, all herbs and Tahini (or oat flakes) and stir until smooth. Boil 2 minutes and purée smooth with a hand blender.

WHITE BEANS AND CELERY TOMATO SOUP
2-4 people

INGREDIENTS:

100 g white beans (or kidney beans), soaked overnight
⅓ celeriac (celery root)
2 stalks of celery
2 carrots
1 parsnip
2 tbsp. tomato paste
1 tsp. kalonji seeds, ground
1 tsp. caraway, ground
1 bay leaf

⅓ tsp. marjoram
½ tsp. turmeric
1 pinch asafetida
½ tsp. coriander powder
1 tsp. salt
¼ tsp. black pepper
1 tsp. raw sugar
1 tsp. ghee
3 tbsp. olive oil
fresh herbs - basil or parsley
4 cups (1 l) of water

PREPARATION:

Wash white beans and simmer for 30 minutes, then drain. Heat the ghee and fry the spices. Add the chopped celery, carrots and parsnip and fry for 1 minute. Add water and beans. Simmer for about 35 to 40 minutes (until the beans are soft).

Finally, add the tomato paste, olive oil, fresh herbs, sugar, salt, and pepper, and bring to a boil briefly.

ROOT VEGETABLES AND GINGER SOUP
2 people

INGREDIENTS:

2 cups mixed root vegetables, peeled and sliced - parsnips, parsley root, celeriac, carrots, potatoes
1 tbsp. grated fresh ginger
½ tsp. cumin, coarsely crushed
½ tsp. coriander, coarsely crushed
½ tsp. turmeric
1 pinch asafetida
1-2 bay leaves
3 cups (750 ml) of water
1 tsp. black salt
1 pinch black pepper, crushed
1-2 tsp. ghee
Fresh herbs to taste

PREPARATION:

Heat the ghee in a saucepan. Fry the cumin seeds until they are brown. Add the root vegetables, ginger, and other spices (except salt) and fry everything together for 1 minute. Add the water and simmer for 25 minutes. Remove the bay leaf.

Finally, add salt and fresh herbs and purée everything with a hand blender.

VEGETABLE COCONUT MILK SOUP WITH SWEET POTATOES & LIME LEAVES
4 people

INGREDIENTS:

2 potatoes, peeled and chopped
2 carrots, peeled and finely chopped
1 big sweet potato
¼ cauliflower, cut into florets
2 tsp. grated fresh ginger
½ red pepper
1 tsp. coriander seeds, coarsely crushed
½ tsp. asafetida
½ tsp. turmeric
¼ tsp. ajwain seeds, coarsely crushed
100 ml coconut milk
4 lime leaves (fresh or deep-frozen, never use dry ones)
1 tsp. black salt
½ lemon, squeezed
1 tbsp. fresh herbs, finely chopped - coriander, parsley or dill
½ tsp. black pepper, ground
4 cups (1 l) of water
2 tsp. ghee or virgin coconut oil

PREPARATION:

Heat the ghee in a saucepan and add the coriander and ajwain seeds. Fry for a few seconds. Now add the vegetables and the remaining powdered spices (asafetida, turmeric), fresh ginger and fry briefly. Pour in the water and simmer for about 25 minutes.

Finally, add the coconut milk, lemon juice, salt, pepper and fresh herbs and purée to a fine consistency with a hand blender or food processor. Now add lime leaves, stir and let the soup rest covered for a while.
Finished!

You can add 1/2 cup cooked chickpeas or other cooked lentils

credits to: Greenmorning

DELICATE RED VEGETABLE SOUP "BORSCHT"
4 people

INGREDIENTS:

2 beets, peeled and cut into small cubes
1/6 white cabbage, finely chopped
1-2 parsnips, peeled and cubed
2 carrots, peeled and cubed
2 potatoes, peeled and diced
⅓ cup (100 ml) tomato purée or
2 tsp. thick tomato paste
1 tbsp. dill, finely chopped
1 tbsp. of sour cream, whisked
1-2 tsp. ghee
½ tsp. asafetida
½ tsp. turmeric
1 tsp. coriander powder
½ tsp. caraway seeds
1-½ tsp. black salt
½ tsp. black pepper
4 cups (1 l) water

PREPARATION:

Heat the ghee in a saucepan, add the beets and fry briefly. Add the caraway seeds, asafetida, turmeric, coriander and fry for a few seconds. Add water, cover and simmer for 20 minutes. Add the rest of the vegetables (except the tomatoes) and simmer for 20 minutes more.

Finally, add the salt, pepper, tomato juice, sour cream, and fresh dill and bring to a boil. Finished!

HOKKAIDO PUMPKIN MUNG DAL CREAM SOUP
2 people

INGREDIENTS:

¼ Hokkaido pumpkin or any other pumpkin with orange flesh
½ cup (125 ml) mung dal, split and dehulled
2 parsnips, peeled and cubed
½ tsp. fenugreek powder
½ tsp. turmeric
1 tsp. ground coriander
⅓ tsp. asafetida
⅓ tsp. black pepper
1 tbsp. fresh coriander, finely chopped
½ lemon, squeezed
2 cups (500 ml) water
1 tsp. salt
1 tsp. ghee

PREPARATION:

Wash the Hokkaido pumpkin, remove seeds and cut into chunks. Wash mung dal and leave covered in water for ½ hour. Heat the ghee in a pan and fry the coriander, turmeric, fenugreek and asafetida briefly, add the pumpkin and parsnips and fry. Add the mung dal, water and bring to a boil. Partially cover and simmer for about 30 minutes.

Finally, add the salt, pepper, lemon juice and fresh cilantro and finely purée everything. Bring to a boil and serve immediately.

Ahimsa Dairy Products

3.

AHIMSA DAIRY PRODUCTS

According to Ayurveda, milk is a very special food that contains everything our body needs: proteins, vitamins and lots of minerals, especially calcium. You could say Milk is an energy bomb. Lets look at which type of milk Ayurveda refers to when recommending it for our health.

In most supermarkets today, we can buy only low-quality, industrially-processed milk from mass production. Cruelty associated with milk production is one of the best kept secrets in the farming industry. The cows from factory farming experience extreme pain, stress and sorrow. Such dairy products bring negative energy to your body and are not easy to digest to say the least. Using such milk (also homogenised or ultra-high heated milk) can cause allergies such as lactose or milk protein intolerance. Factory farming in the western world is far from any ayurvedic values of life and respect towards animals. So big is the contrast that cow in the Far East in Hindu tradition is considered sacred animal and seen as a Mother!

The cow horn is one of cows organs and an important agent when she is producing milk. Most farmers burn the horns when they are calves, which inevitably lowers the quality of milk.
When buying this "miracle drink" you should look to find one in it's purest form and aim for ahimsa kind, which in Sanskrit means "to cause no harm". It is slaughter free and from organic farms, where they keep the cows and their calves together for at least a year and where the cows still have horns. Sounds like time travel to our ancestors land where they were able to have raw and fresh milk from their cows and goats on their breakfast table every day. It was their number one food.
A small cup of warm milk with spices and a few drops of ghee in the evening can be used as medicine as it will nourish your brain cells, nerves and bone tissue. Try to use raw milk (which needs to be boiled) or pasteurised milk. Organic milk not only tastes better but it also has a more positive subtle effect. To scoop all these wonderful benefits of milk, always drink it warm (as warm as possible) and avoid drinking it cold at all costs as it is hard to digest and can cause mucous congestion.
For myself and my family I choose to consume only ahimsa milk, and if that is not available when I am traveling, I obstain from it, having understood how it can have negative effect on my mental and physical health. Choosing kindness and love towards all living beings and sharing my thirty years of experience and understanding of this rich and colourful world of Ayurveda brings me great joy. Bring your food to the frequency that will make you healthy and shine inside and out.

Namaste
Love to all

There are many nondairy options available if you want or need to avoid cow's milk. The best are almond, coconut, cashew und hemp milk. Most of the recipes in this book are made with almond milk.

Good combinations with organic milk are:

milk + spices (e.g., turmeric, black pepper, saffron, ginger, cinnamon, cardamom, nutmeg)
milk + nuts (best are almonds)
milk + (unsulfured) dried fruits
milk + mango
milk + wheat
milk + ghee and raw cane sugar

Bad combinations and combinations that are very hard to digest are:

milk + salt
milk + garlic
milk + eggs
milk + animal protein
milk + fruit or vegetables

Home-made dairy products
(Paneer - White Curd Cheese, Yogurt, and Ghee)

GHEE - AYURVEDIC GOLD
(clarified butter)

According to Ayurveda, ghee is liquid gold. It is Rasayana, a royal, rejuvenating and longevity promoting food. Ghee is free from lactose and milk protein, so it is suitable for people with milk intolerance. The benefits of ghee are countless, so we will mention only a few:

- supports and nourishes brain and nerves cells
- good for digestion
- does not harm the liver, but supports it
- has a cooling effect. Therefore, it is the best for irritated eyes or skin
- keeps the joints healthy
- increase one's immunity and vital energy ojas
- helps to reduce excess stomach acid and maintains/repairs the mucus lining of the stomach
- increases absorption of nutrients and enhances the flavor of foods
- Ghee is the most easily digestible fat, it contains vitamin A and E and it acts as an antioxidant
- When you sauté your spices and herbs in ghee, the lipid-soluble portions of the herbs are carried to the lipid-based cell walls of the body, where they impart the most benefit. Ghee can help protect those cells as well. Most of the digestive enzymes are fat-soluble, and their precursor is fat. Ghee stimulates those enzymes, allowing food to be broken down more efficiently.

HOW TO MAKE GHEE
yield 350-400 g of ghee

INGREDIENTS:

500 g organic unsalted butter

PREPARATION:

Place the butter in heavy saucepan over moderate heat (perhaps even low heat). Be careful, butter can burn very quickly if one is not attentive. Cook over low or moderate heat until the surface of melted butter is covered by heavy, white foam. Carefully remove the thick foam and stir it. From time to time, you will need to do it again. Reduce the heat as low as possible, do not cover and let the water evaporate from the butter. Please be careful that your ghee does not turn brown which means it has burned.

Again remove the foam. After 25-30 minutes your ghee will turn clear and golden. Set aside and let it cool down. Sift through clean kitchen cloth.

Store the ghee at room temperature in a jar, always covered. Ghee can reach 100 years (as it gets older, it becomes more potent).

YOGURT
yields about 1 l yogurt

INGREDIENTS:

1 l milk (at least 3.6% fat)
2 tbsp. yogurt (at least 3.6% fat)

PREPARATION:

Bring the milk to boil. Set aside and wait until the temperature of the milk drop to 45°C. A cooking thermometer is a useful accessory for this recipe. Put the yogurt in the milk and whisk for a few seconds. Cover with pot lid and wrap with 1-2 kitchen cloths. For the next 8 hours, do not move the yogurt pot. After 8-10 hours you can open the pot and change the container. Stainless steel should be replaced with jar or clay pot with a proper lid. Store in fridge (use in 3-5 days).

THE TRUE GOAL OF ACTION IS KNOWLEDGE OF THE SELF.

PANEER (WHITE CURD CHEESE)
yields about 450 g cheese (depends on the milk quality)

INGREDIENTS:

2.5 l milk (at least 3.6% fat)
juice of 2-3 lemons

PREPARATION:

Bring the milk to a rolling boil, stirring frequently. Set aside and very slowly add the lemon juice. It is possible that you will not need it all. The milk should immediately separate into lumps of curd (on the surface) and whey underneath. Whey liquid should be yellow-green in colour.

Line a colander with cheesecloth or just some clean kitchen cloth and place it over one pot to collect the whey. Pour the whole liquid with lumps of curd in the kitchen cloth. Take the four corners of cloth and tie them together. Gently squeeze the rest of liquid out of the curds.

Place the paneer cheese under some weight (e.g., a pot full of water) until firm. It will take 20-30 minutes.

Voilà, you made beautiful cheese all by yourself!

95

Rice Dishes

4.

credits to Greenmorning

RICE DISHES
A small grain with a big impact

Rice feeds more people around the world than any other grain. It is lighter than wheat and oats, and more versatile than any other cereal.

One can make pulaos, loafs, casseroles, pancakes, simple side dishes or sweet puddings with rice. It is a staple food that contains many essential amino acids and, in combination with lentils, dairy products or nuts, can serve as a complete protein source. Basmati rice is the king of all varieties of rice, especially for its aroma and fragrance. It is easy to digest, cooling and ideal in the summer and for Pitta types. Whole grain rice is very earthy and harder to digest. It is recommended for healthy individuals with a strong digestion. Rice noodles are lighter than wheat or spelt pasta and taste great. Rice flour can be used for puddings, cakes and pancakes. It is best if you grind the rice at home. If you do not have a grain mill, you can use a small coffee grinder.

We offer in this book a simple and quick method for cooking rice. Wash the rice, drain at least 20 to 30 minutes and fry in a little ghee until the rice is soft. Then add the water and salt, stir only one time, cover and simmer for 15 minutes. It is very important not to stir the rice while cooking, as it will burn.

If you have no time to drain the rice after washing, you can roast it dry (directly from the package) in ghee. Draining the wet rice is very important as the wet rice falls apart and sticks during roasting and is therefore not suitable for this cooking process. Brown rice does not need to be roasted. Pour it gently into the boiling water, with or without salt, and let it simmer without stirring until the rice has absorbed all the water and is tender (about 25 minutes).

If you add a few pieces of vegetables, nuts or lentils to the rice, you will get a deliciously well-rounded, light and nutritious lunch.

BASMATI RICE NATURAL
3-4 people

INGREDIENTS:

1 cup (250 ml) basmati rice
2 cups (450-500 ml) water
½ tsp. salt
1 tsp. ghee

PREPARATION:

It is advisable to wash the basmati rice. If you're in a hurry, you can also use unwashed rice. If you wash rice, let the rice drain at least 20 minutes before roasting. The rice should be completely dry. Otherwise, it falls apart when frying, which is not desirable. Heat the ghee in a pan with a thick bottom. Add basmati rice and fry slowly, about 2 minutes, stirring constantly. Once the grains are translucent, pour in the salt and water. Stir once, so that the salt is distributed evenly, and cover well. The cover should fit perfectly.

Simmer about 12 to 15 minutes without stirring (otherwise the rice will burn). The rice should be tender, with the grains separated from each other, and all the water should be absorbed. It is best to let the rice for rest covered for 10 minutes (off the burner).

PUSH PANNA (FLOWER RICE WITH NUTS AND VEGETABLES)
3-4 people

INGREDIENTS:

1 cup basmati rice
1-½ cups water
1 cup mixed vegetables – broccoli, carrots, celery, zucchini
1 handful of toasted cashews
4 cardamom pods
4 cloves
1 tsp. ground coriander
½ tsp. turmeric
½ tsp. asafetida
1 eggplant (aubergine) cut into cubes and toasted or grilled (optional)
1-2 tsp. ghee
1 tsp. salt

PREPARATION:

Heat up the ghee in a saucepan. Fry the spice seeds, add the rice and fry for about 2 minutes. Add the spice powder and roast. Add the water, vegetables and salt, cover and simmer for about 12-15 minutes. Do not stir until the end. Set aside. Let the rice rest covered for 10 minutes.

Stir and add the roasted cashews and eggplant.

LEMON BASMATI RICE
4 people

INGREDIENTS:

1 cup (250 ml) basmati rice
2 tsp. ghee
7 curry or lime leaves
½ tsp. turmeric
2 tbsp. lemon juice
1 tsp. salt
2 cups (500 ml) water

PREPARATION:

Rinse the rice 3 times and let drain in a colander for 30 minutes. Heat the ghee in a pan over medium heat and sauté the curry leaves briefly. Add the rice, fry for 2 minutes on low heat, then add the turmeric and fry for a few seconds more. Then add the water and salt, stir once, cover and bring to a boil. Cover and cook on low heat for 12 minutes (do not stir, because the rice could burn).

Set aside and allow the rice to rest for another 5-10 minutes, covered. Sprinkle with lemon juice, stir and serve.

SPICY BASMATI RICE WITH GRILLED EGGPLANT AND ROASTED CASHEW NUTS
3-4 people

INGREDIENTS:

1 cup (250 ml) basmati rice
2 cups (500 ml) water
1 tsp. ghee for the rice
1 eggplant (aubergine) diced
100 g roasted cashews
1 tsp. coriander powder
½ tsp. turmeric
½ tsp. asafetida
½ tsp. garam masala
1 tbsp. raisins (optional)
2 tbsp. fresh cilantro, finely chopped
1 pinch of chili powder
⅓ tsp. paprika
1 tsp. salt for rice
½ tsp. salt for eggplant (aubergine) and cashews
sunflower oil for frying

PREPARATION:

Roast or grill the eggplant in a frying pan with a little olive oil or ghee, add salt and set aside briefly. Heat up the ghee in a saucepan. Fry the spice seeds, add the rice and fry for about 2 minutes. Add the spice powder and roast. Add the water, vegetables and salt, cover and simmer for about 12-15 minutes. Do not stir until the end. Set aside. Let the rice rest covered for 10 minutes.

Stir and add the roasted cashews and eggplant.

RICE WITH TOMATOES, PEPPERS, AND PINE NUTS
2 people

INGREDIENTS:

1 cup (250 ml) basmati rice, rinsed and dry (strained) – Arborio or long-grain rice can be substituted
2 tomatoes, finely chopped
1 red or green bell pepper, finely chopped
50 g pine nuts
½ tsp. caraway seeds
½ tsp. asafetida
½ tsp. turmeric
1 tsp. salt
2 tbsp. fresh herbs to taste – basil, dill, parsley
1 tsp. ghee
1 ½ cup (400 ml) water
1 pinch black pepper

PREPARATION:

Roast the pine nuts in a frying pan with a little olive oil and set aside briefly. Heat up the ghee in a saucepan and add caraway seeds and rice. Fry about 2 minutes and then add the asafetida and turmeric and fry for a few seconds. Pour the water, tomato, black pepper, salt and bell pepper and stir again. Cover and simmer for about 12 to 15 minutes, until the rice has absorbed all the water.

Finally, let the rice stand for 10 minutes uncovered, then gently fold in the fresh herbs and pine nuts.

SAFFRON RICE WITH ALMONDS AND SUGAR SNAP PEAS
2-3 people

INGREDIENTS:

1 cup (250 ml) basmati rice
2 cups (500 ml) water or whey
70 g almonds, whole, peeled and toasted
10-15 pieces of saffron threads, crushed in a mortar to powder and mixed with
4 tbsp. of hot water
1 tsp. salt
150 g sugar snap peas, cut into julienne strips / or just green peas
⅓ tsp. asafetida
4-5 cloves
1 bay leaf
2 tsp. ghee

PREPARATION:

Heat up the ghee in a saucepan, add the rice, cloves, asafetida and bay leaf and fry 2 minutes until translucent. Add the water or whey. Add the salt and sugar snap peas and stir one time gently. Cover and simmer over low heat about 12 to 15 minutes. Set aside for 10 minutes to rest.

Take the lid off the pan and remove cloves and bay leaf and pour the saffron essence (powdered saffron threads mixed with hot water). Stir in toasted almonds gently.

SESAME RICE WITH GREEN BEANS, CARROTS, AND TOFU (NATURAL OR SMOKED)
4 people

INGREDIENTS:

1 cup (250 ml) basmati rice (or another type of rice)
250 g fresh green beans, diagonally sliced into small pieces
2 carrots cut into strips
3 tbsp. sesame seeds (sunflower seeds can be used as a replacement)
2 cups (500 ml) water
2 tsp. ghee
1 tsp. salt
½ tsp. asafetida
½ tsp. turmeric
½ tsp. coriander powder
½ tsp. garam masala
½ lemon, squeezed
100 g smoked tofu, cubed

PREPARATION:

Add the tofu to the pan and fry briefly until it is golden brown, add sesame seeds and fry for another 2 minutes. Put aside. Heat the ghee in a saucepan and add the rice. Fry the rice slowly, stirring constantly (about 2 minutes). Now add the asafetida, coriander and turmeric and fry for a few seconds more. Pour the water, salt and vegetables and stir once. Cover well and simmer for about 15 minutes without stirring.

Finally, fold in the tofu, sesame seeds, garam masala and lemon juice and let the rice rest covered for 10 minutes.

BASMATI RICE PULAO WITH CAULIFLOWER AND YOGURT MASALA

3-4 people

INGREDIENTS:

1 cup (250 ml) basmati rice
1 ½ cup (400 ml) water
120 ml plain yogurt
2 cups cauliflower, chopped
2 tbsp. grated coconut
1 tbsp. fresh ginger, finely grated
1 tbsp. fresh herbs - parsley or coriander
½ tsp. turmeric
⅓ tsp. brown mustard seeds
⅓ tsp. cumin seeds
3 green cardamom pods
2 tsp. ghee
2 tbsp. sunflower oil
1 tsp. salt - ½ tsp. salt for the rice –
½ tsp. for yogurt and cauliflower

PREPARATION:

Heat the sunflower oil in a wok and add the cauliflower. Fry until golden brown and then put to the side. Mix the desiccated coconut, yogurt, fresh herbs, turmeric, salt and fresh ginger together. Add the cauliflower. Heat up the ghee in a saucepan, fry mustard seeds and cumin (with the cover on) briefly until the mustard seeds pop and turn gray. Add the basmati rice and fry for another 2 minutes until translucent.

Add the water, salt and cardamom pods and simmer covered for 12 minutes. Carefully fold in the yogurt-masala-cauliflower mixture and simmer covered for another 3 to 4 minutes. Let rest for 10 minutes.

BROWN RICE WITH BROWN LENTILS AND VEGETABLES
4-5 people

INGREDIENTS:

1 cup (250 ml) brown rice
¼ cup (50 ml) brown lentils
2 carrots, peeled and cut into sticks
1 red pepper, cut into strips
100 g Hokkaido pumpkin or sweet potatoes, chopped
3 cups (700-750 ml, depend on rice) water - for the rice
100 g young spinach, cut into strips
½ tsp. of asafetida
½ tsp. turmeric
1 tsp. coriander seeds, coarsely crushed
½ tsp. fenugreek powder
1 chili pepper, chopped
½ tsp. garam masala
1 tsp. salt
⅓ tsp. ground black pepper
1 tsp. ghee
4-5 tbsp. olive oil

PREPARATION:

Rinse the brown rice and drain. Heat the ghee in a pan and add the coriander, asafetida, turmeric, fenugreek and chili and fry briefly. Add 700-750 ml of water and salt and bring to a boil. Add the rice, cover, and simmer about 25-35 minutes on low heat. When the rice is cooked, it should have absorbed all the water and should be soft. Meanwhile, steam the pumpkin, peppers and carrots briefly in salted water (about 5 minutes), add the spinach strips and steam for another 2 minutes. Drain the vegetables well and set aside. You can also fry the vegetables or stir fry in a wok. In a separate pot, add the brown lentils, 1 tsp. salt and one liter of water. Simmer for about 20-30 minutes, until tender. Drain well.

After the rice, vegetables and lentils are finished cooking, mix them together carefully and add in olive oil, pepper, and garam masala.

Lentils & Legumes

5.

LENTILS AND LEGUMES
A small, round source of high-quality protein

Lentils, beans, pulses and dal (peeled and split lentils) are together, with cereals, the most important staple foods worldwide. They contain many essential minerals, vitamins and trace elements, such as iron, magnesium, potassium, phosphorus and vitamins A, E and B complex in them. In combination with carbohydrates, such as rice or other grains, they provide the body with all essential amino acids (those which the body cannot produce).

Shelled beans or lentils are more digestible than unpeeled. The best lentils or dal are mung dal (peeled and split mung beans) that taste excellent and have a very good effect on the human body. Mung dal is purifying and uplifting, does not cause bloating and it cleanses the body. In the unpeeled form, the mung lentils are green; when peeled, they have a beautiful golden yellow color. The recipes in this book always refer to peeled, split mung beans.

The lentils have bitter or astringent taste, which also acts as a weight-reducing aid. Our modern diet rarely includes lentils, but Ayurveda recommends, depending on the constitution and digestion, that vegetarians should eat lentils at least three to five times a week. Vata types should always eat lentils with spices that counteract against flatulence. The lentil dishes should have a splash of lemon juice added before serving. For Pitta and Kapha types, lentils are ideal.

BLACK BEANS/
BROWN CHICKPEAS

BROWN LENTILS/
CHANA DAL

CHICKPEAS/
MEDITERRANEAN
BEANS

MOONG BEANS/
MOONG DAL

URAD DAL/
WHITE BEANS

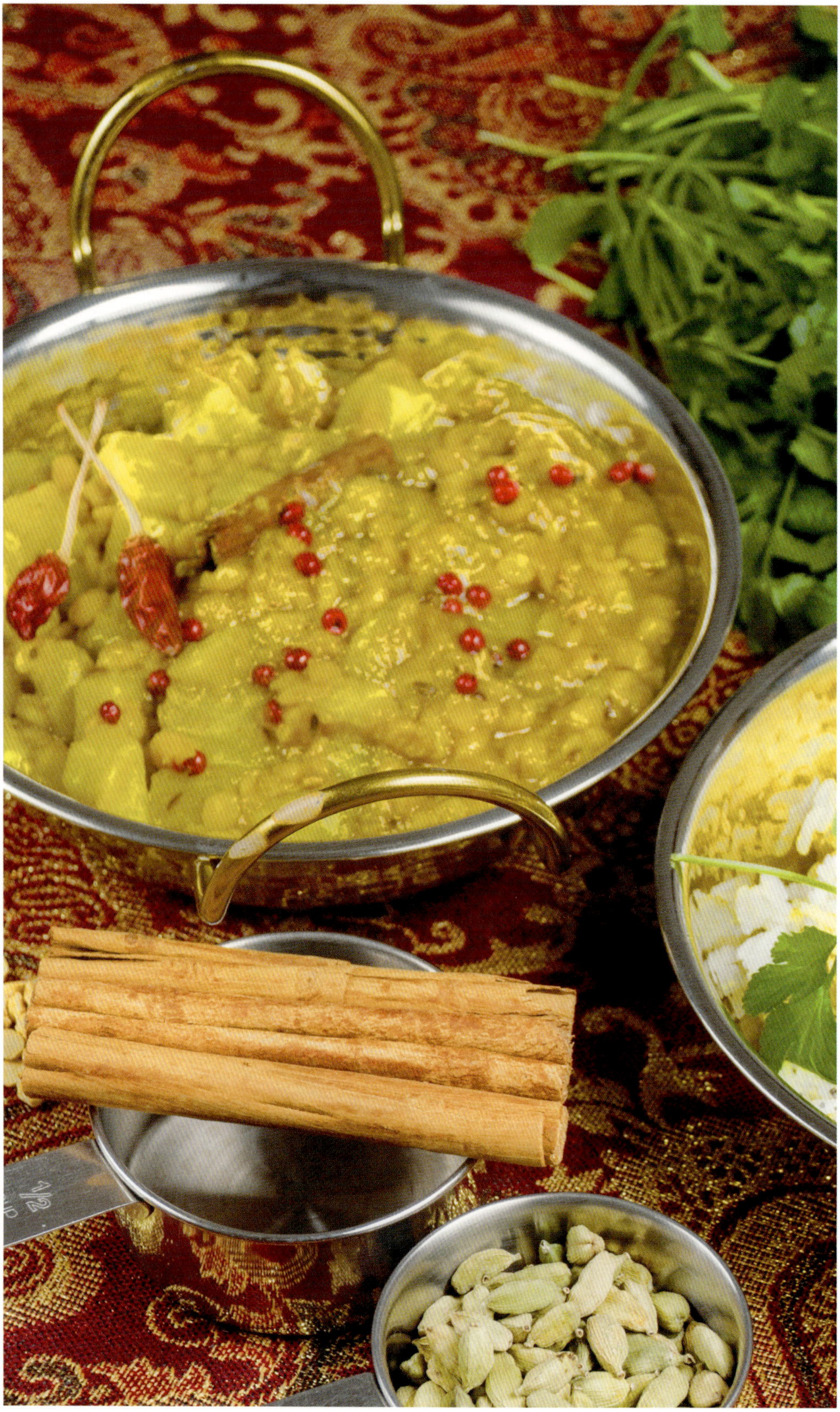
1/2

ALU CHANA DAL (SPLIT CHICKPEAS - LENTILS WITH POTATOES)
4 people

INGREDIENTS:

1 cup (250 ml) chana dal –
split and peeled
chickpeas – soaked overnight
or at least for one hour
1 cinnamon stick
2 potatoes, peeled and diced
1 tsp. fennel seeds
1 tsp. coriander seeds
1 tsp. fresh ginger
½ tsp. turmeric
⅓ tsp. asafetida
½ lemon, squeezed
1 tsp. salt
Fresh herbs to taste

PREPARATION:

Wash the dal three times and place in a heavy saucepan with ¾ l of water. Bring the water to a boil and skim off the foam. Simmer for about 10 minutes, then add the potatoes and cinnamon stick and then cook for another 20 minutes. Meanwhile, heat 1 tsp. ghee in a small saucepan and fry the coarsely crushed coriander and fennel seeds in it. Then, add the ginger, turmeric, and asafetida and fry a little. Now add the masala to the dal and add salt, lemon juice and fresh herbs to taste.
 Finished!

Try whole Mung bean instead of Chana Dal (also soaked in water over night).
Mung has the special quality of being nourishing for the tissues and immune system (due to its sweetness) but also light and easy to digest.

WARM LENTIL VEGETABLE SALAD
3-4 people

INGREDIENTS:

200 g brown lentils (soak for at least 1-2 hours)
2 carrots, peeled and cut into matchsticks
⅓ celeriac, peeled and cut into matchsticks
½ red pepper, chopped
1 fennel, finely chopped
1 tsp. tomato paste
½ tsp. dried basil
⅓ tsp. dried thyme
⅓ tsp. asafetida
⅓ tsp. turmeric
⅓ tsp. black pepper
⅓ tsp. red chili powder
½ tsp. caraway seeds, ground
4 tbsp. olive oil
3 tbsp. balsamic vinegar or the juice of 1 lemon, squeezed
1 tsp. raw cane sugar
1 ½ tsp. salt
2 tbsp. fresh herbs to taste
2 tbsp. sesame oil

PREPARATION:

Drain the brown lentils, rinse well, and place in a saucepan with 1 liter of water and bring to a boil. Simmer until the lentils are very soft but not overcooked (about 30 minutes). Rinse with cold water and drain. Wash the vegetables and cut into sticks. In a wok, heat 2 tbsp. sesame oil and fry the vegetables until they are golden-brown. Heat olive oil in a pan and fry turmeric, asafetida, cumin and paprika for a few seconds, then add the tomato paste and fry another 10 seconds. Pour in the lentils and vegetables and mix well with the tomato paste. Add the balsamic vinegar, fresh herbs, salt, sugar, pepper, basil and thyme. Finished! This salad can be enjoyed hot or cold.

SAMBAR DAL - STOVE VEGETABLE STEW
3-4 people

INGREDIENTS:

200 g chana dal (split chickpeas), soak at least 2 hours or overnight
¼ Hokkaido pumpkin
1 red pepper
1 eggplant
1 zucchini
3 tomatoes
1 lemon, squeezed
2 tbsp. fresh cilantro, finely chopped
1 cinnamon stick

1 tsp. coriander seeds, coarsely ground
½ tsp. cumin seeds, coarsely ground
½ tsp. black mustard seeds
½ tsp. fenugreek, ground
½ tsp. of asafetida
1 tsp. turmeric
½ tsp. black pepper
1 tbsp. ghee
1 tsp. salt
2 cups (500 ml) water
100 ml coconut milk (optional)

PREPARATION:

Place the chana dal in a saucepan with 700 ml water and bring to a boil. Cook until the lentils are tender (about 30-40 minutes). Rinse with cold water and drain. Heat up the oven to 250° C (482° F). Wash the vegetables. Do not peel eggplant and Hokkaido pumpkin, but cut into 3 cm pieces and place in a baking pan. Drizzle some olive oil and sprinkle ½ tsp. salt. Bake about 15 minutes. Cut the zucchini into thick slices and the peppers into cubes, add to baked vegetables and bake for another 7 minutes. Cut the tomatoes into cubes and remove the seeds. Heat a large pan with 1 tbsp. of ghee, pour in the mustard seeds, cover and wait until they stop jumping. Immediately add the caraway seeds and coriander seeds and roast. Then add the cinnamon stick, turmeric, asafetida and fenugreek and roast for a few seconds.

Add the lentils and the tomatoes to the spice mixture and simmer for 15 minutes. Finally, add the baked vegetables with fresh coriander, lemon juice, salt, and pepper and stir gently.

MOUSSAKA – POTATO-EGGPLANT AND LENTIL CASSEROLE
6–8 people

INGREDIENTS:

1 kg potatoes
100 g brown lentils
2 large eggplants (aubergines), sliced
2 zucchinis (courgettes), cut oblong
2 tbsp. tomato paste or 200 ml tomato, strained
50 g Parmesan cheese, grated
50 g sunflower seeds for sprinkling
1 tsp. sweet paprika
1 tsp. cumin, ground
2 tbsp. ghee or sunflower oil
3 tbsp. olive oil
1 tsp. salt for the potatoes
⅔ tsp. salt for the lentils
1 tsp. coriander, ground

½ tsp. oregano
½ tsp. basil
⅓ tsp. thyme
½ tsp. asafetida
½ tsp. turmeric
1 tsp. mixed salad herbs
1 chili, finely chopped
1 tsp. raw sugar

BÉCHAMEL SAUCE:

3 tbsp. olive oil
2 tbsp. flour
500 ml almond milk
1 tsp. salt
¼ tsp. black pepper

olive oil in a saucepan and add the flour. Fry for 1-2 minutes on low heat. Add the almond milk. Stir the sauce with a whisk quickly so that no lumps form. Add ⅔ tsp. salt and stir continuously until the Béchamel sauce is cooked. Put aside.

PREPARATION:

Heat up 1 tbsp. of ghee in a pan and fry 4-5 eggplant slices on both sides about 2 minutes. Fry zucchini in the same manner. Drain well. Cook the brown lentils in about 700 ml of water until soft (about 25 minutes). Drain well. Cook 1 kg potatoes with the skin until soft, peel and cut into slices. Combine 3 tbsp. olive oil, 1 tsp. salt, chili, pepper, and cumin and add to the sliced potatoes, stirring gently.

In a saucepan, heat 1 tsp. ghee and fry the coriander, turmeric, and asafetida over moderate heat. Add the basil, thyme, oregano, salad herbs and tomato paste and fry slowly for 30 seconds. Add the soft cooked lentils and 100 ml water and simmer for 10 minutes. Finally, add salt, pepper and sugar and set aside.

For the Béchamel sauce, heat up 3 tbsp.

PREPARING THE MOUSSAKA:

Brush a deep baking dish (about 20 x 30 cm) with olive oil. Place 1 layer of potato slices (⅓ of the potatoes) evenly into the pan, then add half the eggplant and zucchini and a little salt. Then add half of the lentil stew and sprinkle with ⅓ of the Parmesan cheese. Repeat everything in the next step: potatoes (⅓), eggplant (aubergines) and zucchini (courgettes) (½), lentil stew (½) and Parmesan (⅓). Add the final ⅓ of the potatoes to the casserole and pour the Béchamel sauce evenly over the top. Sprinkle the casserole with the remaining Parmesan and sunflower seeds.

Bake at 180°-200°C (356°-392° F) for 30 minutes.

AYURVEDIC CLASSICS - KITCHARI RICE, DAL, AND VEGETABLE STEW

Kitchari is probably the most famous Ayurvedic classic. Whether it is cooked for breakfast, lunch or for various cleansing and detox cures, kitchari is always delicious. This stew of grain, dal and vegetables contains all the nutrients that our bodies need. The composition of protein, carbohydrates, minerals, vitamins and trace elements makes it a perfect food. Kitchari is easy and can be prepared in 30-45 minutes. If you add some salad and yogurt mixed with a few fresh herbs and salt, you can have a great lunch!

There are countless kitchari recipes, simply vary the ingredients that you have at home. For example, instead of mung dal, you can substitute chana dal, red/brown/green lentils, or use toor dal (yellow lentils). Rice can be replaced by barley, millet, buckwheat, bulgur wheat or quinoa.

KITCHARI 1 - WITH COLORED VEGETABLES
2 people

INGREDIENTS:

50 g mung dal - yellow lentils
(soaked for one hour or overnight)
70 g basmati rice
1 cup chopped vegetables - carrots,
broccoli, bell pepper
1-2 tsp. ghee
¾ l water
1 tsp. black salt (kala namak)
fresh herbs to taste
½ lemon, squeezed

Spice mix:
½ tsp. cumin seeds, coarsely crushed
½ tsp. turmeric powder
½ tsp. coriander powder
½ tsp. fenugreek powder
⅓ tsp. asafetida
a little fresh grated ginger
½ tsp. black pepper
1 cinnamon stick

PREPARATION:

Rinse rice and dal well and bring to a boil in ¾ liter of water with a cinnamon stick. Skim the foam off and simmer for 15 minutes. Add the vegetables, adding the ones that require a longer cooking time first, such as carrots or green beans. Cook over low heat 10 minutes. Do not cover the kitchari, as the lentils might tend to overcook. Stir often. Now add the vegetables with short cooking times such as cauliflower or zucchini. In a small saucepan, heat the ghee and fry the cumin seeds until they are brown. Pour in other spices and fresh ginger and fry another 5-10 seconds. Pour the finished masala in the pot with rice, dal and vegetables and garnish with salt, herbs and lemon juice. Finished!

TIP 1: Cut fresh spinach coarsely and mix in at the end
TIP 2: Bake potatoes in the oven, and add at the end
TIP 3: Add a little coconut milk

KAPHA: It is better to replace the rice with millet, quinoa or buckwheat.

"Kitchari" contains all essential nutrients. It is rich in iron, B vitamins and high-quality protein. Since it is easily digested, it is highly recommended for all constitutions.

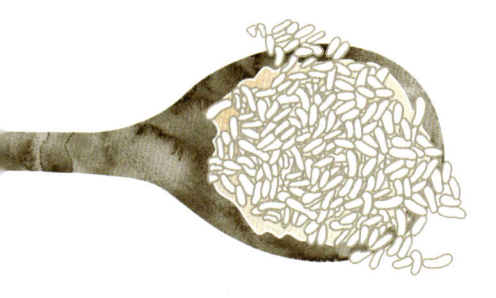

KITCHARI 2 - WITH SPINACH AND POTATOES
2 people

INGREDIENTS:

50 g mung dal
50 g basmati rice - or long grain or short grain rice
200 g spinach leaves
2 potatoes
1 tsp. coriander seeds, coarsely crushed
½ tsp. fenugreek powder
½ tsp. garam masala
1 tsp. turmeric
⅓ tsp. asafetida
½ tsp. ajwain seeds, coarsely crushed
1 tbsp. fresh ginger, finely grated
⅓ tsp. ghee
1 tsp. black salt (kala namak)
1 pinch black pepper
½ lemon, squeezed

PREPARATION:

Wash the spinach leaves, drain well and cut into large strips. Peel, wash and dice the potatoes. Rinse the mung dal and basmati rice well and bring to a boil in a pot with 500 ml water. Skim off the foam and simmer for 10 minutes without a lid. Add the potatoes and cook for another 20 minutes. If necessary, add a little water. Stir often.

In a small pan, heat the ghee and add the coriander seeds and ajwain seeds. Fry until they are brown. Add the turmeric, asafetida and ginger and fry for a few seconds. Add the toasted masala to the stew. Add the coarsely chopped spinach leaves, salt, pepper, garam masala and lemon juice into it and simmer for another 5 minutes until the stew thickens.

Serve it with raw vegetables and a dollop of yogurt.

KITCHARI 3 – PULAO RICE, DAL, AND VEGETABLES FROM THE WOK
2 people

INGREDIENTS:

50 g yellow chana dal lentils - or yellow lentils (soaked in water, preferably overnight or at least one hour)
100 ml basmati rice
¼ Hokkaido pumpkin
1 red pepper
½ broccoli
1 piece fennel
2 tomatoes, chopped
3 tbsp. soy sauce
2 tbsp. sesame seeds
1 tsp. ghee
2-3 tbsp. cold-pressed sesame oil
1 tsp. salt
1 tsp. ground coriander
½ tsp. turmeric
½ tsp. asafetida
1 tsp. curry powder
⅓ tsp. mild black pepper
2 tbsp. fresh herbs to taste, finely chopped

PREPARATION:

Wash the chana dal and cook in 1 l of water until the lentils are tender. Rinse in cold water, drain and add a little salt. Wash basmati rice well and drain at least 20 minutes. In a saucepan, heat 1 tsp. ghee and fry the dry rice for 2 minutes until it is soft. Pour 190 ml of water in, add salt, stir once, cover and simmer 15 minutes. The rice should have absorbed all the water and the grains should be loose. Remove from heat and let stand covered for 10 minutes.
Wash all vegetables and cut into strips.

Heat 2-3 tbsp. sesame oil in a wok and add the vegetables (except tomatoes). Cover and sauté at medium to high heat for about 10 minutes, stirring occasionally. Add the coriander, turmeric, pepper, sesame seeds and asafetida, cook briefly and deglaze with soy sauce. Add the tomatoes and simmer covered for another 5 minutes. Finally, add the rice, dal, pepper, curry powder and fresh herbs and stir gently. This dish goes well with a salad and flatbread.

Subjies & Curries

6.

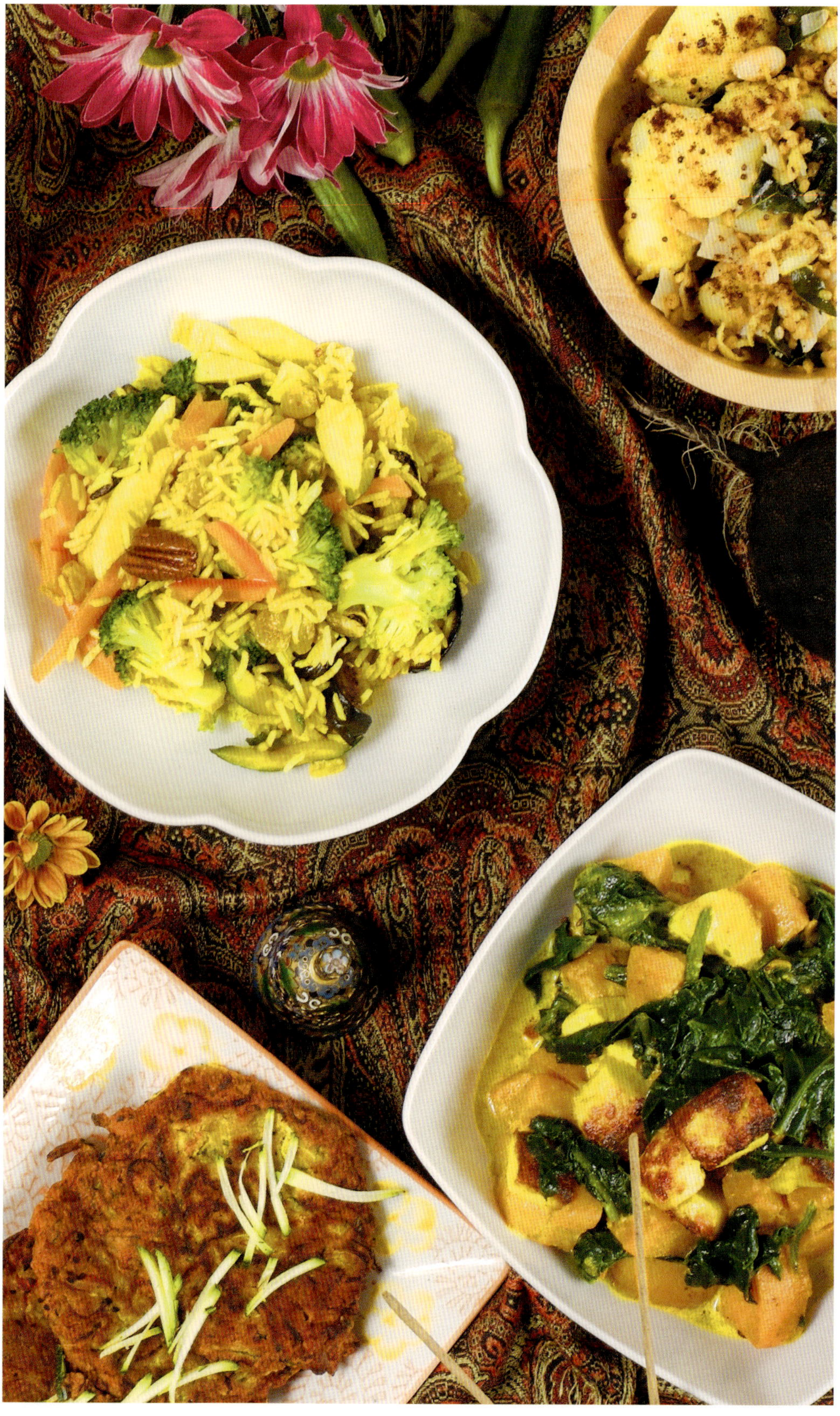

SUBJIS: CURRIES AND VEGETABLE DISHES
Cooked, steamed, stir-fried

"Vegetable" is a term for a wide variety of foods. The colors, shapes, smells and flavors may overwhelm us and you will be surprised about the many possibilities. The Ayurvedic cooking offers hundreds of different vegetable dishes and cooking methods, which leave nothing to be desired. The proper spices can highlight the taste of vegetables. Whether steamed, baked, or stir-fried in a wok, vegetables always taste excellent when prepared properly. The recipes in this book show us which spices fit together with which vegetables and the best way to prepare a dish that tastes outstanding. In combination with grains, lentils or nuts, vegetables belong to a good Ayurvedic meal. The original vegetable dishes were called subjis. Later, when India was a British colony, subjis were called curry. Both terms are used when referring to a vegetable dish.

By adding coconut milk, a little heavy cream, or yogurt a subji can be very creamy. By baking in an oven, the vegetables are spicier and slightly richer. Stewing or steaming a curry or subji makes it lighter and easily digestible. In combination with a paneer, the curry is more substantial and filling and by adding lots of fresh herbs, such as coriander, gives it somewhat bitter taste.

Fresh vegetables cannot be compared to frozen ones. Although frozen vegetables contain vitamins, the prana, or life force, is no longer available. As often as possible, you should buy fresh organic vegetables. Frozen vegetables cannot compare to the taste of fresh ones.

Many vegetables have a healing effect on the body. Artichokes, for example, aid liver function. Asparagus helps to build up the blood. Potatoes are alkaline. Pumpkin and sweet potatoes help to build and strengthen body tissues. Spinach and chard purify the blood and liver and help prevent cancer. Carrots are very good for the eyes. Beets are also blood-building. All vegetables are helpful in lowering cholesterol.

COLORFUL VEGETABLES IN COCONUT MILK SUBJI
3-4 people

INGREDIENTS:

1 cup (about 150 g) potatoes, chopped
1 cup pumpkin, chopped
1 cup broccoli, chopped
½ red pepper and 1 small piece fresh ginger, place them in a food processor to make a paste
⅓ cup (100 ml) coconut milk
1 tsp. cumin, coarsely crushed
1 tsp. coriander, coarsely crushed
½ tsp. turmeric
⅓ tsp. asafetida
1-2 tsp. ghee
1 tsp. black salt (kala namak)

PREPARATION:

Heat the ghee in a saucepan, add the cumin seeds and fry for 30 seconds over moderate heat until the cumin has turned brown. Add coriander, turmeric and asafetida, fry for a few seconds. Add pumpkin, potatoes and the ginger-red pepper paste and fry another 30 seconds. With a little water, deglaze and simmer 15 minutes. Add the broccoli and little water and cook for another 5 minutes. Finally, season with coconut milk and salt. Depending on your taste, you can add cooked chickpeas or fried homemade cheese (paneer). The vegetable mix can vary according to the season.

OKRA BELL PEPPER SUBJI WITH MUSTARD SEEDS
2-3 people

INGREDIENTS:

400 g young okra (lady´s fingers)
1 red bell pepper
1 tsp. black mustard seeds
⅓ tsp. asafetida powder
½ tsp. turmeric
½ tsp. coriander powder
1 tsp. salt
3 tbsp. sesame oil or virgin coconut fat

PREPARATION:

Wash the okra and drain well. Heat the sesame oil in a heavy pan. Saute the mustard seeds, add okra, cover and stir fry on a moderate heat for 10 minutes. Stir occasionally. Add all spices and sauté for an additional 5 minutes. Finished!

GREEN BEANS, CARROT AND PEPPER SUBJI
3-4 people

INGREDIENTS:

2 cups (about 300 g) green beans
2 carrots
1 red pepper
2 tbsp. white poppy seeds
¾ cup (200 g) yogurt
1 tsp. grated ginger
8-10 curry leaves or 1-2 bay leaves
1 pinch of nutmeg powder
½ tsp. cumin seeds
1 tsp. turmeric
⅓ tsp. asafetida
1-½ tsp. salt
1 tbsp. ghee
1 pinch of chili powder

PREPARATION:

Wash the green beans, carrots, and peppers and cut into strips. Heat the ghee, fry the cumin over moderate heat for 30 seconds, and then fry ginger and curry leaves. Add the vegetables and cover with 150 ml of water and let simmer for 20 minutes. Meanwhile, grind the white poppy seeds and mix well with yogurt and chili. Finally, stir everything together and season with salt and nutmeg.

SWEET POTATO, SPINACH AND PANEER SUBJI
4 people

INGREDIENTS:

500 g spinach, washed, well drained and roughly chopped
500 g sweet potatoes, peeled and sliced
100 g paneer (homemade curd cheese) (see page 94)
1 tsp. ghee
1 tsp. ground coriander
1 tsp. fenugreek seeds
1 tsp. turmeric
½ tsp. asafetida
⅓ cup (100 ml) heavy cream or coconut milk
1 tsp. salt
⅓ cup (100 ml) water

PREPARATION:

Heat the ghee in a saucepan over medium heat and fry the spices for few seconds. Add the sweet potatoes and fry for another 2 minutes. Pour water over it and simmer for about 15 minutes. Meanwhile, slice the paneer cheese into small cubes and fry until golden brown in a frying pan (or you can use unroasted paneer). Salt lightly. Add the spinach to the sweet potatoes and simmer for 3 minutes.

Finally, add cream, paneer and salt and bring gently to boil.

130

SPICY POTATO NUT STEW
4 people

INGREDIENTS:

1 kg (10 pieces) waxy potatoes
1 cup (100 g) cashew nuts (or shelled almonds)
4 tbsp. grated coconut
2 tbsp. urad dal, peeled
1 tsp. black mustard seeds
2 chilies, finely chopped
½ tsp. asafetida
1 tbsp. ghee or 2-3 tbsp. virgin unroasted sesame oil
1 lemon, squeezed
2-3 bay leaves
1 pinch of ground nutmeg
1 tsp. salt
black pepper to taste

PREPARATION:

Cook the potatoes in a pot until they are tender. Rinse well with cold water and let cool. Peel the potatoes and cut into 0.5 cm thick slices or cubes. In a wok, heat the ghee, fry the mustard seeds while covered until they no longer pop. Add the urad dal, grated coconut and cashews, fry over moderate heat for a few seconds until the dal and nuts turn a golden brown color. Add the chilies, ginger, bay leaves, and asafetida and fry for a few seconds. Now add potatoes and fry for about 4-5 minutes. Finally, add salt, black pepper, nutmeg and pour the lemon juice over the top. Finished!

GLAZED COLORFUL VEGETABLES FROM THE WOK WITH TOFU AND SOY SAUCE
4-6 people

INGREDIENTS:

2 carrots peeled and cut into matchsticks
1 bunch mangold (Swiss chard), cut into strips
100 g mung bean sprouts (optional)
100 g sugar snap peas or green beans, cut into 2.5 cm long rods
1 red or yellow bell pepper, cut into strips
1 zucchini, sliced thinly on the diagonal
½ broccoli, cut into small florets
10 cm piece of leek (cut into strips)
250 g smoked tofu or plain tofu, cut into strips
1-½ tsp. coriander seeds, coarsely crushed
1 tbsp. grated fresh ginger
½ tsp. ground cumin
½ tsp. asafetida
1 tsp. red or green chilies, finely chopped with seeds removed
1 bunch fresh coriander, finely chopped
¼ cup (80 ml) soy sauce
1 tbsp. tomato paste
1 tsp. cornstarch
100 ml water
1 tsp. chili sauce, sweet and sour
2-3 tbsp. sesame oil
1 tbsp. sunflower oil

PREPARATION:

Steam the carrots, sugar snap peas/green beans and broccoli briefly in a little water. Heat the oil and fry the tofu. Set aside. Stir the tomato paste with soy sauce, cornstarch, water, chili sauce until smooth. In a wok, heat the sunflower oil and fry the crushed coriander seeds, asafetida, chili, grated ginger and ground cumin and fry briefly. Add the leek, mangold, bean sprouts and zucchini and fry for about for 2-3 minutes in the wok. Now pour in the soy-cornstarch mixture and bring to the boil gently, while stirring constantly.

Add the steamed carrots, sugar snap peas, broccoli, sesame oil, fresh coriander and tofu and cook briefly to a boil. The vegetables should have a fine glazed coating and a beautiful shine.

Serve with rice noodles!

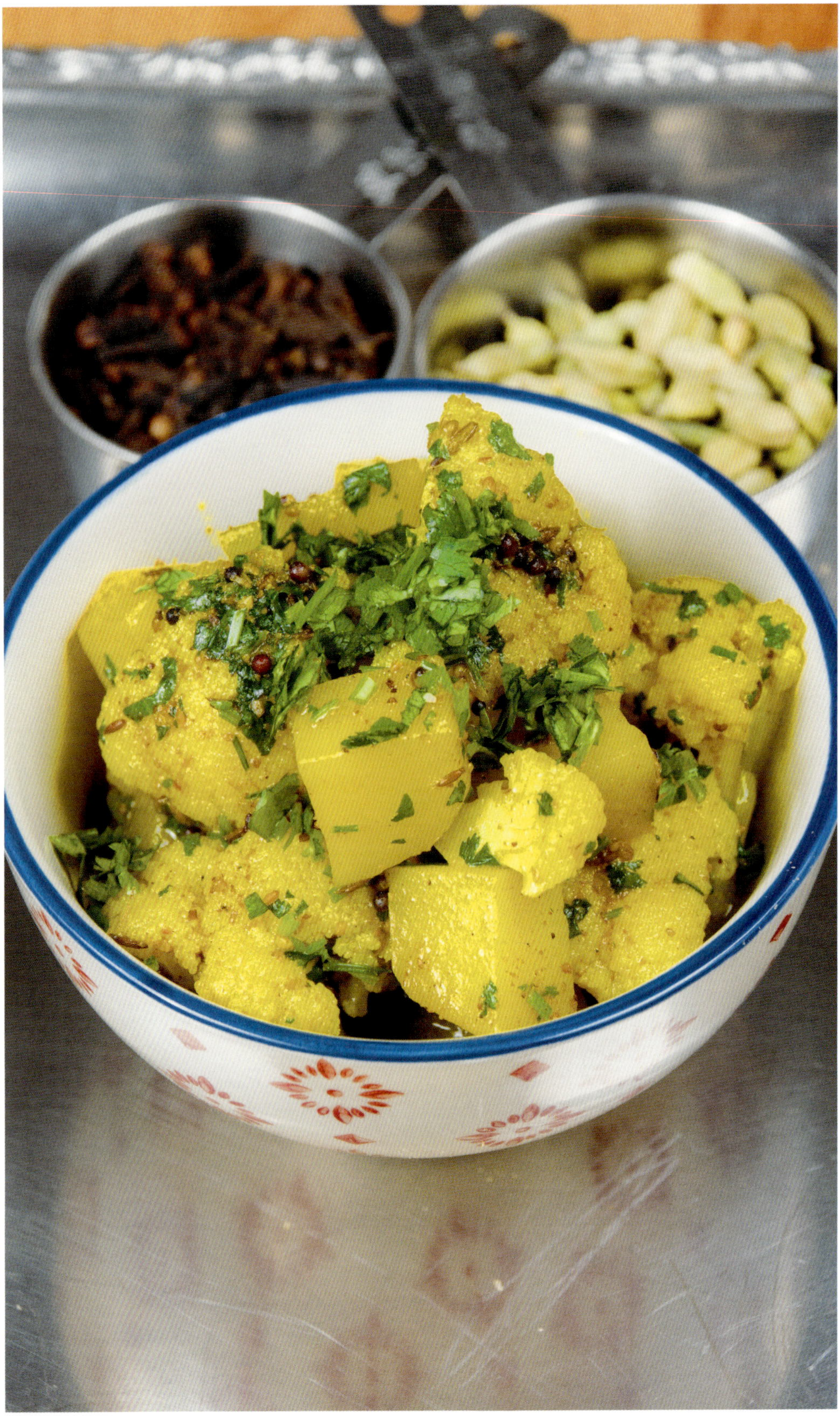

CAULIFLOWER AND POTATO SUBJI
4 people

INGREDIENTS:

1 small cauliflower, cut into florets
2-3 potatoes, cut into cubes
1 tbsp. grated fresh ginger
½ tsp. cumin seeds
½ tsp. black mustard seeds
⅓ tsp. asafetida
½ tsp. turmeric
½ tsp. ground coriander
½ tsp. garam masala
1 tsp. black salt (kala namak)
½ lemon, squeezed
1 tbsp. fresh herbs finely chopped - parsley or coriander
1-2 tsp. ghee or virgin coconut fat
about ⅔ cup (150 ml) of water

PREPARATION:

Heat the ghee in a saucepan and add mustard seeds. Cover the pot and wait until the seeds are no longer popping. Lower the heat, add the cumin seeds and fry until they turn brown. Now pour in the well-drained potato cubes and fry briefly. Add the ginger, coriander, turmeric and asafetida and fry for a few seconds with the roasted potatoes. Now add the water, cover the pot, and simmer for 10 minutes. Add the cauliflower florets, cover and cook over moderate heat for about 10 minutes. Continue to simmer until the vegetables are cooked. It is important not to stir too often, as it breaks down the vegetables very quickly. If the water has already evaporated, add a little more.

Finally, add the garam masala, salt, lemon juice and fresh herbs, stir briefly and bring to a boil. Turn off the flame and let it rest covered for 10 minutes.

BAKED BEETROOT WITH POTATOES AND CAULIFLOWER IN HERB-NIGELLA SEEDS-SAUCE
4 people

INGREDIENTS:

2-3 beets
4 potatoes, peeled and cubed
½ head cauliflower cut into florets
3 tbsp Tahini sesame seed paste (Thin the dressing with a little more water, if necessary.)
1 tsp. curry powder
⅓ tsp. asafetida
1 tsp. coriander powder
1 tsp. nigella seeds (kalonji or black cumin seeds)
½ tsp. sweet paprika powder
fresh herbs - cilantro, parsley or dill
1 tsp. salt
2 tsp. ghee or 3-4 tbsp. virgin sunflower oil

PREPARATION:

Wash the beets, cover with water, and cook covered for about 1 hour until soft. Peel and dice the cooked beets. Sprinkle with a bit of salt and set aside. Put the potatoes into a bowl and season with 1 tsp. ghee, ½ tsp. salt, asafetida, half of the coriander and paprika. Place the mixture in a baking pan and bake in preheated oven, 220° C (428° F) about 10 minutes. Put the cauliflower in a bowl with 1 tsp. ghee, ½ tsp. salt, nigella seeds and the half of the coriander and paprika. Add the cauliflower to the potatoes in the oven and bake for another 20 minutes until golden.

Finally, lay the beets in the baking pan and garnish the dish with Tahini dressing, curry powder and fresh herbs.

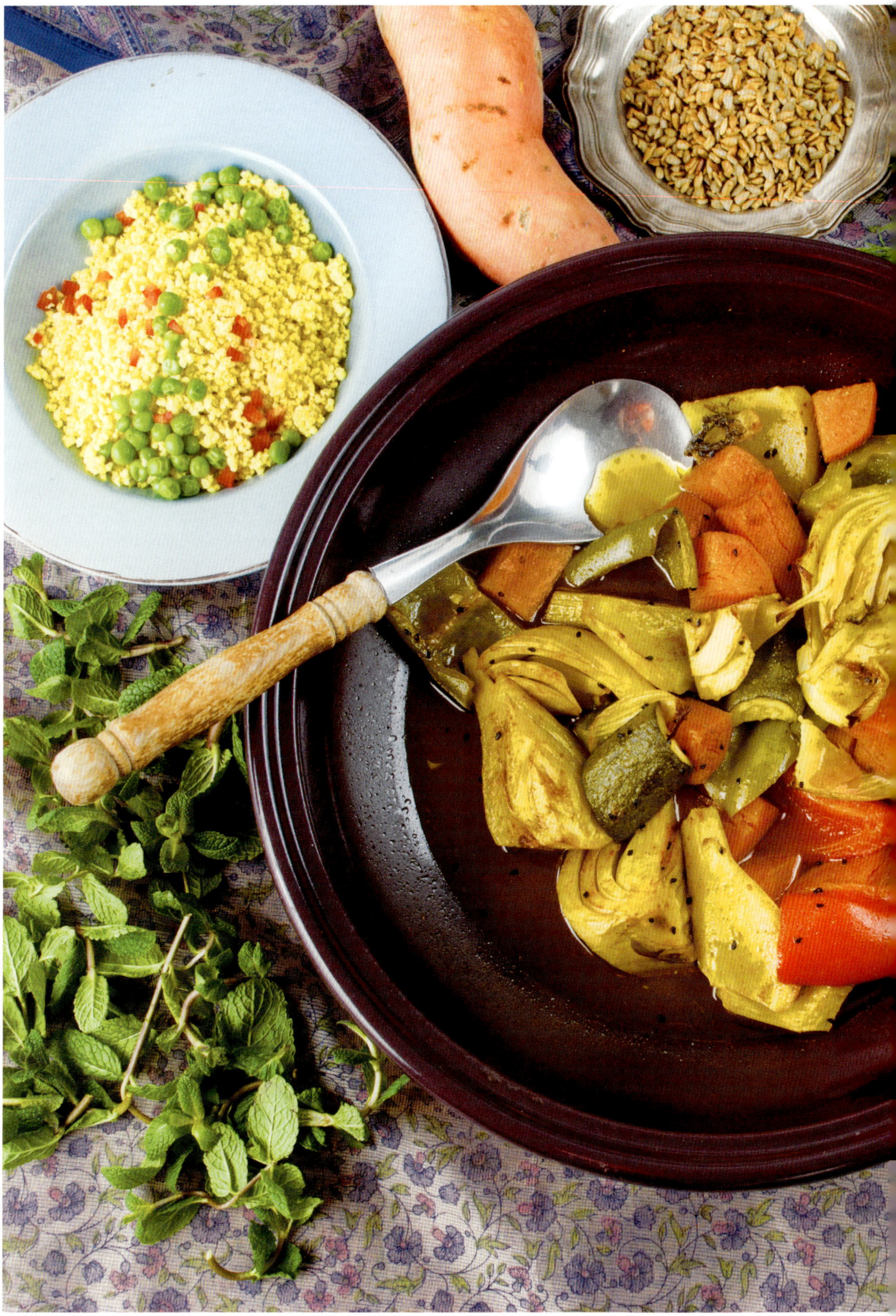

OVEN-BAKED VEGETABLE CURRY IN TAGINE (MOROCCAN COOKING VESSEL)

4 people

INGREDIENTS:

2 eggplants (aubergines), cubed
2 fennel bulbs, cut into big pieces
3 potatoes, peeled and diced
2 red peppers, cut into thick strips
2 tomatoes, cubed
1 tsp. nigella seeds
1 tsp. coriander powder
1 tsp. turmeric
1 tsp. sweet red paprika powder
1 tbsp. fresh coriander, finely chopped
1-½ tsp. salt
2 tsp. ghee or virgin olive oil
½ tsp. black pepper
100 ml water

PREPARATION:

Preheat the oven to 160° C (320° F). Mix all ingredients in the tagine, close and bake for 1 hour and 30 minutes. Delicious!

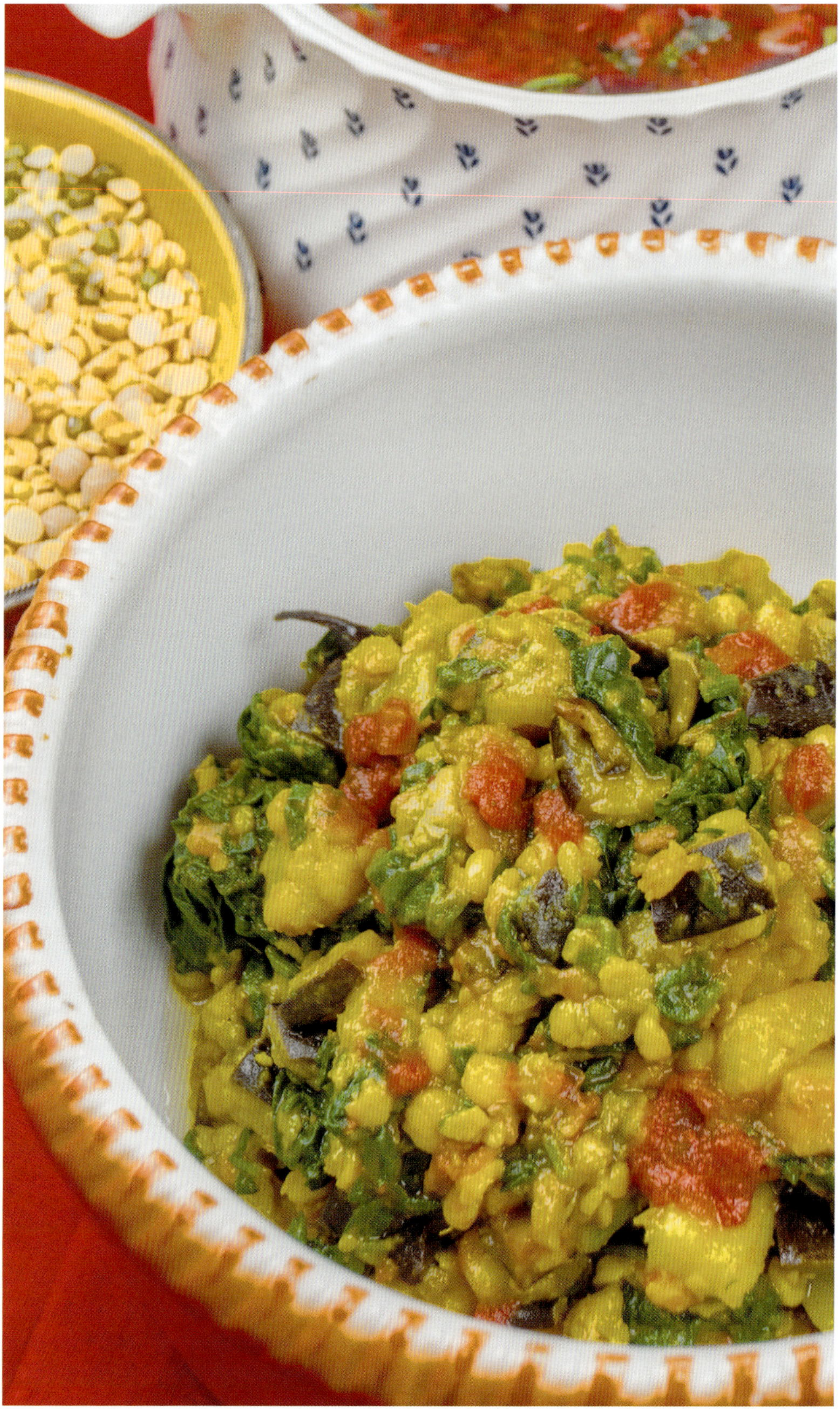

CREAMY SPINACH, EGGPLANT AND YELLOW LENTILS
4 people

INGREDIENTS:

350 g fresh spinach, washed, well drained and coarsely cut into strips
1 cup (100 g) chana dal, soak overnight or for at least two hours
(you can use any type of lentils)
2 eggplants (aubergines), cut into large cubes
2 tbsp. thick tomato paste or ⅔ cup (180 ml) of tomato juice
1-½ tsp. coriander seeds, coarsely crushed
½ tsp. asafetida
1 tsp. turmeric
1 tsp. fenugreek, ground
1-½ tsp. salt
1 stick of cinnamon
2 tsp. ghee - for masala
3 tbsp. olive oil - for eggplants (aubergines)
1 tbsp. grated fresh ginger
1 tsp. sweet paprika powder
½ tsp. salt - for eggplants (aubergines)
1 tsp. raw sugar

PREPARATION:

Place the chana dal in about 700 ml of boiling water and simmer for 30 minutes. Drain well. Dal must be soft so that it will crush easily between 2 fingers. Place the eggplant cubes in a bowl, season with salt, pepper and olive oil and mix well. Place the cubes in a baking pan (casserole). Set the oven to 220° C (428° F) or place under a broiler. Bake the eggplant for about 15-20 minutes. It must be buttery soft at the end and not tough. In a large saucepan, heat the ghee, add the coriander seeds, ginger, asafetida, turmeric, fenugreek and cinnamon stick and fry for a few seconds over moderate heat. Add the spinach and pour in about 150 ml (⅔ cup) of water and simmer for 2 minutes. Now add the chana dal, tomato paste, sugar, baked eggplant and salt and stir gently. Subji should have a thick consistency (not too dry and not too runny). Simmer 5 minutes more, cover and turn off the flame. Let it rest for about 10 minutes.

ZUCCHINI, POTATO AND PEPPER SUBJI
3 people

INGREDIENTS:

2 small zucchini, cubed
2-4 potatoes, peeled and cubed
1 red or green bell pepper
1 tbsp. grated fresh ginger
⅓ tsp. asafetida
½ tsp. turmeric
1 pinch black pepper
½ tsp. ground coriander
½ tsp. ground cumin
1 tsp. black salt (kala namak)
1-2 tsp. ghee
2 tbsp. fresh herbs - parsley, dill or cilantro
½ lemon, squeezed
about 2/3 cup (150 ml) of water

PREPARATION:

Heat the ghee in a saucepan and fry the spices for few seconds over moderate heat. Add the potatoes and peppers and fry for a few seconds. Now pour the water in, cover and simmer for 15 minutes. Add the zucchini and simmer for another 3 minutes.

Finally, add salt, pepper, fresh herbs and lemon, turn off the flame, cover, and let it rest for 10 minutes.

POTATO PANEER GRATIN "GAURANGA"
6 people

INGREDIENTS:

700 g waxy potatoes, peeled and thinly sliced
250 g paneer or feta cheese, thinly sliced (see page 94)
¾ cup (200 ml) heavy cream
1 tsp. coriander seeds, coarsely crushed
1 tsp. turmeric
½ tsp. asafetida
1 tsp. salt - for potatoes
½ tsp. black pepper
2-3 tbsp. virgin sunflower oil

PREPARATION:

Drain the potatoes well, mix immediately with salt, coriander, asafetida, pepper and turmeric and divide into three parts. Divide the sliced paneer into 2 parts. Coat a deep baking dish (casserole) with ghee or oil and sprinkle the first layer of potatoes on it. Place the paneer slices next and add a bit of salt. Then repeat the process again. Put the third layer of potatoes on top. Pour the heavy cream evenly over the top and gently cover with aluminum foil.

Bake the gratin in the oven for about 30-45 minutes at 200° C (392° F). During the last 10 minutes, you can remove the foil and continue baking until the top turns golden brown.

FENNEL, POTATOES, AND MANGOLD (CHARD) IN COCONUT MILK SUBJI WITH HOMEMADE CHEESE PANEER
4 people

INGREDIENTS:

2 fennel bulbs, cut into strips
2-3 potatoes, cut into strips
250 g mangold (chard), cut into strips
150 ml coconut milk
1 tbsp. fresh ginger, finely grated
½ red pepper, grated in a food processor (you can do it together with the ginger)
½ tsp. cumin seeds
½ tsp. coriander, ground
½ tsp. fenugreek, ground
½ tsp. asafetida
½ tsp. turmeric
½ tsp. black pepper
150 g paneer, cubed (optional) (see page 94)
1-½ tsp. salt
1 tsp. tomato paste
1 tsp. ghee
150 ml water

PREPARATION:

Heat the ghee in a saucepan and fry the cumin over moderate heat until brown. Add the coriander, fenugreek, turmeric and asafetida and fry for a few seconds. Add the well-drained potatoes and fennel, add grated pepper and ginger and continue to fry briefly. Pour the water and simmer covered for 10 minutes. Add the mangold, tomato paste, coconut milk, salt and black pepper and simmer covered for another 10 minutes.

Finally, add in the diced paneer and stir. Instead of paneer cheese, you can use some roasted nuts. Finished!

OVEN-BAKED VEGETABLE CURRY
4 people

INGREDIENTS:

2 eggplants (aubergines), cubed
2 zucchini (courgettes), thickly sliced
3 potatoes, peeled and diced
2 red peppers, cut into thick strips
2 tomatoes, cubed
1 tsp. cumin powder
1 tsp. coriander powder
1 tsp. turmeric
1 tsp. sweet red paprika powder
1 tbsp. fresh coriander, finely chopped
1-½ tsp. salt
2 tsp. ghee or virgin olive oil
½ tsp. black pepper

PREPARATION:

Mix all of the powdered spices with salt in a bowl. Preheat the oven to 220° C (428° F). First, sprinkle the eggplant cubes with ⅓ of the spice mixture and stir in 2 tsp. of ghee. Spread the eggplant in a baking pan (casserole) and place it into the hot oven. Bake for about 10 minutes. Sprinkle the potatoes and peppers with ⅓ of the spice mixture and stir in 1 tsp. of ghee. Then, add the potatoes and peppers to the eggplant pieces, stir one time. Bake another 15 minutes. Sprinkle the zucchini and tomatoes with ⅓ of the seasoning mixture, add to the baking vegetables and bake for an additional 5-10 minutes.

The vegetables should finally be golden brown and caramelised.

GREEN BEANS, CARROTS, AND POTATOES IN A DELICIOUS KADHY SAUCE
2-3 people

INGREDIENTS:

2 cups (250 g) green beans, cut into 2.5 cm long strips
2 carrots, peeled and cut into matchsticks
2-3 potatoes, peeled and cubed
½ red pepper, grated
2 tbsp. chickpea flour (gram flour or besan)
¾ cup (200 ml) plain yogurt
1.5 cup (400 ml) water
10 curry leaves (optional - lime leaves can be used)
1 tbsp. grated fresh ginger
1 tsp. turmeric
½ tsp. black mustard seeds
⅓ tsp. asafetida
1 tsp. coriander powder
½ tsp. cumin seeds
1 tsp. ghee
1 tsp. salt
1 chili, seeded and finely chopped
2 tbsp. fresh herbs - parsley or coriander

PREPARATION:

Steam the green beans, carrots and potatoes briefly in a little water until they are al dente. Drain well. Mix the yogurt, cooking water (about 400 ml), and chickpea flour well, until the mixture is smooth. Heat the ghee in a saucepan, add mustard seeds, cover and wait until the seeds no longer jump. Immediately add the cumin and fry over moderate heat until brown. Lower the flame and pour in all the other spices, ginger, chili and grated bell pepper and fry for a few seconds. Pour the chickpea flour and yogurt mixture into the masala and bring to a boil, stirring constantly. Add the steamed vegetables, salt and fresh herbs and let it thicken for 2 minutes. Subji should have a creamy consistency.

Flatbreads

7.

FLATBREADS
Simple or filled – always a highlight

Bread is not simply bread. In Europe, we are used to eating bread made with yeast. In Asia, flatbreads are usually baked without yeast or with baking soda. These flatbreads are not durable and are eaten warm and fresh. Fresh chapati bread, with a simple or savory filling, is an excellent accompaniment to rice, vegetables, lentils and lettuce. The water quantities indicated in the recipes may vary a little according to the composition of the flour. Most flatbreads are fried in a heavy pan made of cast iron or stainless steel. There is a variety of flatbreads like Chapati, Phulka, Thepla, Roti, Paratha, Bhatura and Puri. In this cookbook, you will find a tasty flatbread that suits you.

The most important thing to remember is to knead the dough smoothly and evenly until you get a nice shiny ball. You may need a little practice when rolling the bread out. Don't give up if your flatbread is not quite round or too thick or thin. Practice makes perfect!

CHAPATI - GRIDDLE-BAKED BREAD (FLAT BREAD WITHOUT YEAST)

6 people

INGREDIENTS:

1 ½ cup (250 g) whole-grain spelt or wheat flour
½ cup (130-150 ml) of warm water (about or as needed)
½ tsp. salt
butter or ghee for brushing on the finished flatbreads

PREPARATION:

In a large bowl, combine flour, salt and water to form a uniform dough, which is not too soft and not too hard. Place the dough on a clean work surface and knead for 2-3 minutes until smooth. Wrap the dough in a damp cloth and let it rest for half an hour. Shape the dough into a snake and cut it into 12 equal pieces. Shape the pieces into balls, sprinkle with a little flour and roll out with a rolling pin as thin and round as possible. Tap off the excess flour and place the chapatis (2-3 at a time) into a preheated heavy skillet. Fry on each side for about 1 minute while stroking the dough surface gently with smooth tongs. This creates small bubbles in the dough. Pick up the chapati with tongs and place it on an open gas flame. The chapati will inflate like a balloon. Immediately turn it over after 2-3 seconds and then set aside.

Store the finished chapati in a suitable pan or basket, brush with ghee or butter and cover the pan to keep the chapatis warm. If possible, serve warm and fresh.

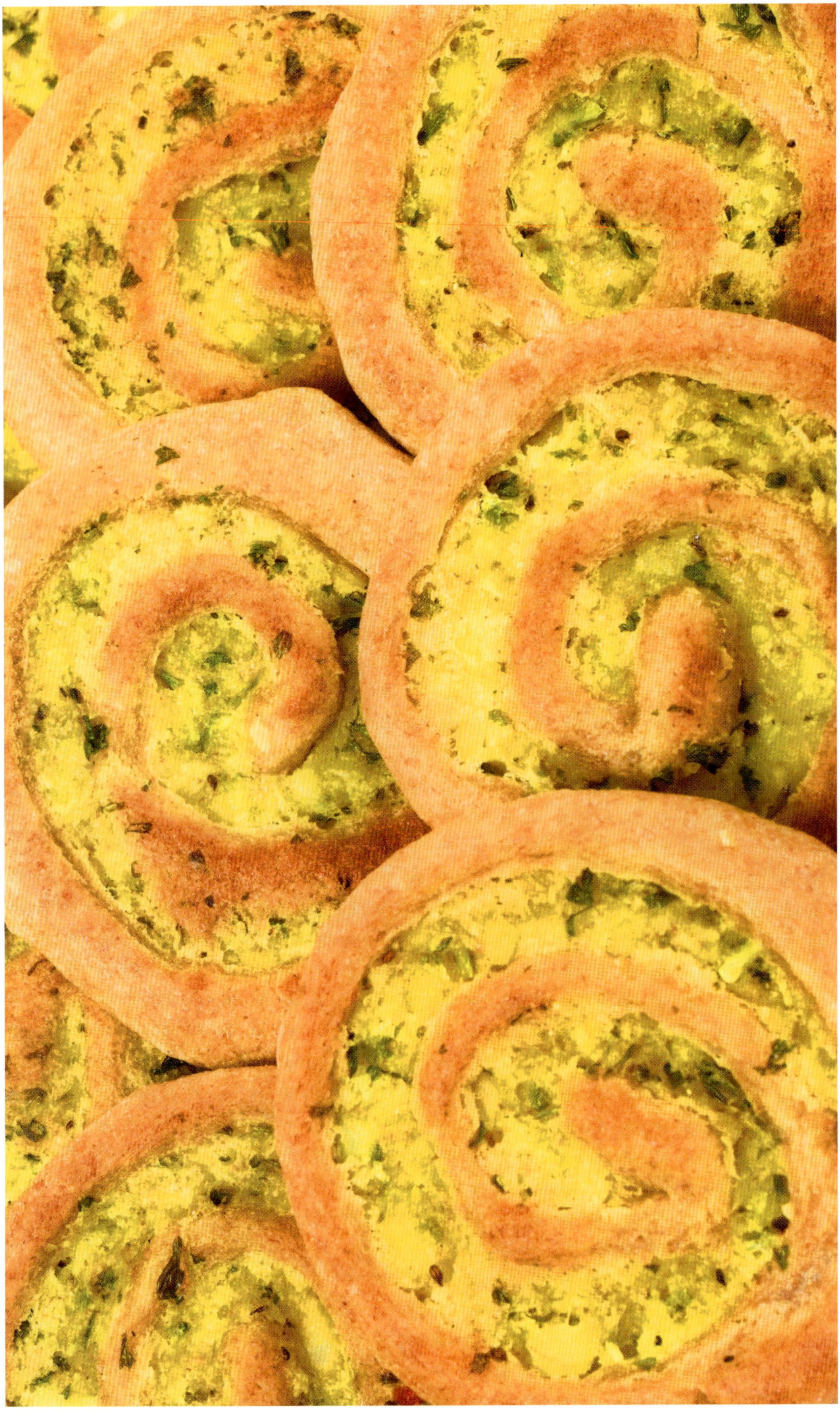

ALOO PATRA - SPICY POTATO SPELT ROULADE WITH GRATED COCONUT, LEMON AND AJWAIN SEEDS

6-8 people

INGREDIENTS:

1 cup (150 g) whole-grain spelt or wheat flour
⅔ cup (100 g) unbleached cake flour
70 g butter or coconut fat
1 tsp. salt – for the dough
½ tsp. baking soda
½ tsp. black pepper
¾ cup (150-180 ml) water

400 g mealy potatoes
1 tbsp. grated fresh ginger
1 tsp. turmeric
½ tsp. ground coriander
½ lemon, squeezed
1 chili, finely chopped
2 pinches asafetida
½ tsp. ajwain seeds, coarsely crushed
1 tbsp. fresh parsley, finely chopped
1 tsp. salt – for the filling
1 tsp. cornstarch
sunflower oil for griddle frying

PREPARATION:

Place the flour, baking powder, salt and pepper in a bowl and mix in the butter with your fingertips. Pour in the water (not all at once, only as much as needed). Knead the dough until it is smooth. Cover with a kitchen towel and let it rest for 20 minutes. Peel the potatoes and boil them in a pot with about ½ liter of water until they are soft. Put the potatoes in a colander, drain well, and let cool. Save the potato water for the soup.

Put the potatoes in a bowl and mix with all the spices, fresh herbs, cornstarch, salt and lemon juice. Mash the potatoes by hand using a masher. It is not recommended to use a hand blender or food processor. Sprinkle a little flour on the work surface and roll out the dough into a square (about 3 mm thick). Spread the potato filling evenly and leave 1 cm free at the edges. Brush the dough on the edges with a bit of water so that it will adhere better and roll the roulade carefully into a tight, thick curl. Cut the roulade into about 1 cm thick slices and shape it firmly with your palms a little. Heat up some sunflower or sesame oil in a pan (just to cover the bottom of the pan), add 3-4 slices of roulade and fry over low or moderate heat on both sides until golden brown (it will take about 3-5 minutes for one side). The burner should be on low heat, otherwise, your roulade slices will burn. Fry all the slices in the same way and serve immediately.

BHATURA WITH BLACK PEPPER AND CORIANDER
(GRIDDLE-FRIED PLAIN FLATBREAD WITH BAKING SODA)
6 people

INGREDIENTS:

1,5 cup (250 g) whole-grain flour – wheat or spelt
50 g butter or coconut fat
1 tsp. salt
½ tsp. black pepper
1 tsp. coriander, coarsely ground
⅔ cup (150 ml) of water or yogurt
½ tsp. baking soda
sunflower oil for griddle frying

PREPARATION:

Soften the butter at room temperature. In a bowl, add the flour, baking soda, salt, pepper, coriander and butter and mix it evenly using your fingers. Now pour the water slowly in and then knead the dough. The dough should not be too soft and not too hard and should not stick to the work surface. Form the dough into a ball, cover with a kitchen towel, and let it rest for 15 minutes. Roll the dough into a snake shape and cut into 16 equal pieces with a knife. Form the pieces into balls and roll out into thin circles, about 3 mm thick. In a skillet, heat some oil (just to cover the bottom) and fry 3-4 Bhaturas over moderate heat on each side until golden brown. Serve immediately.

PANEER PARATHA FILLED WITH PANEER (HOMEMADE CHEESE) OR FETA
6 people

INGREDIENTS:
½ cup (100 g) whole-grain flour – spelt or wheat
1 cup (150 g) unbleached cake white flour
50 g butter or 1 tbsp. ghee
½ tsp. of baking powder
⅔ cup (130-150 ml) of water
100 g paneer (feta cheese can be substituted) (see page 94)
1 tsp. curry powder
½ tsp. salt – for the cheese

PREPARATION:

In a large bowl, mix both kinds of flour and butter with your fingers. Add the baking powder, salt, and water now and knead the dough on a floured work surface. The dough should be smooth and not sticky. Cover the dough with a kitchen towel and let it rest 20 minutes. Crumble the paneer with your fingers and mix with salt and curry powder (if you use feta cheese, do not add salt). From the dough, form 16 balls. Roll out the dough into 15 cm wide circular shapes. In the middle of the circle, brush a little ghee, and then put 1 tsp. of filling in the middle so that you have free edges. Close the dough over the filling. This should form a half-moon shape. Gently roll out the dough with a rolling pin as thin as possible, being careful that the stuffing does not fall out. Then fold the dough into a triangle and roll it out, but not too thin. Fill all 16 patties in this way and roll out.

In a large skillet, heat 1 tbsp. of ghee and fry 2 to 3 parathas at a time, over low heat, each side for 2-3 minutes, until golden brown. Serve immediately.

ALOO PARATHA - PUFF FLATBREAD WITH POTATO FILLING
6-8 people

INGREDIENTS:

⅔ cup (100 g) whole-grain flour – spelt or wheat
1 cup (150 g) unbleached cake flour
50 g butter or coconut fat
½ tsp. of baking powder
½ tsp. salt
⅔ cup (130-150 ml) water
2-3 potatoes, peeled and coarsely chopped

½ tsp. salt – for potatoes
½ tsp. Ajwain seeds, coarsely crushed
⅓ tsp. asafetida
½ tsp. turmeric
⅓ tsp. black pepper
½ tsp. coriander, coarsely crushed
½ lemon, squeezed
1 red chili, seeded and chopped
1 tbsp. fresh herbs – parsley or coriander
Ghee for griddle frying

PREPARATION:

In a large bowl, mix both kinds of flour and crumble the butter into the flour with your fingers. Add the baking powder, salt, and water and form balls of dough with it. The dough should be smooth and not sticky. Cover with a kitchen towel and let it rest for 20 minutes. Cook potatoes until soft in a pot with 2 cups (500 ml) of water. Drain well. In a small pan, heat 1 tsp. ghee and add the ajwain and coriander. Roast until they are brown. Then add the turmeric and asafetida, fry briefly, and remove from heat. Mash the potatoes well, together with toasted spices, salt, fresh herbs, pepper, chili and lemon juice.

   Divide the dough into 16 balls and roll into circular 15 cm wide patties. Brush a little ghee in the middle of each patty. Then add 1 tbsp. of filling in the middle and close the dough over the filling. This should make a half-moon shape. Gently roll out the dough as thin as possible, without letting the stuffing fall out. Fold the dough into a triangle and roll it a bit more. Fill all the patties in this way. In a large skillet, heat 1 tbsp. ghee and fry 2-3 parathas at a time, until they are golden brown.

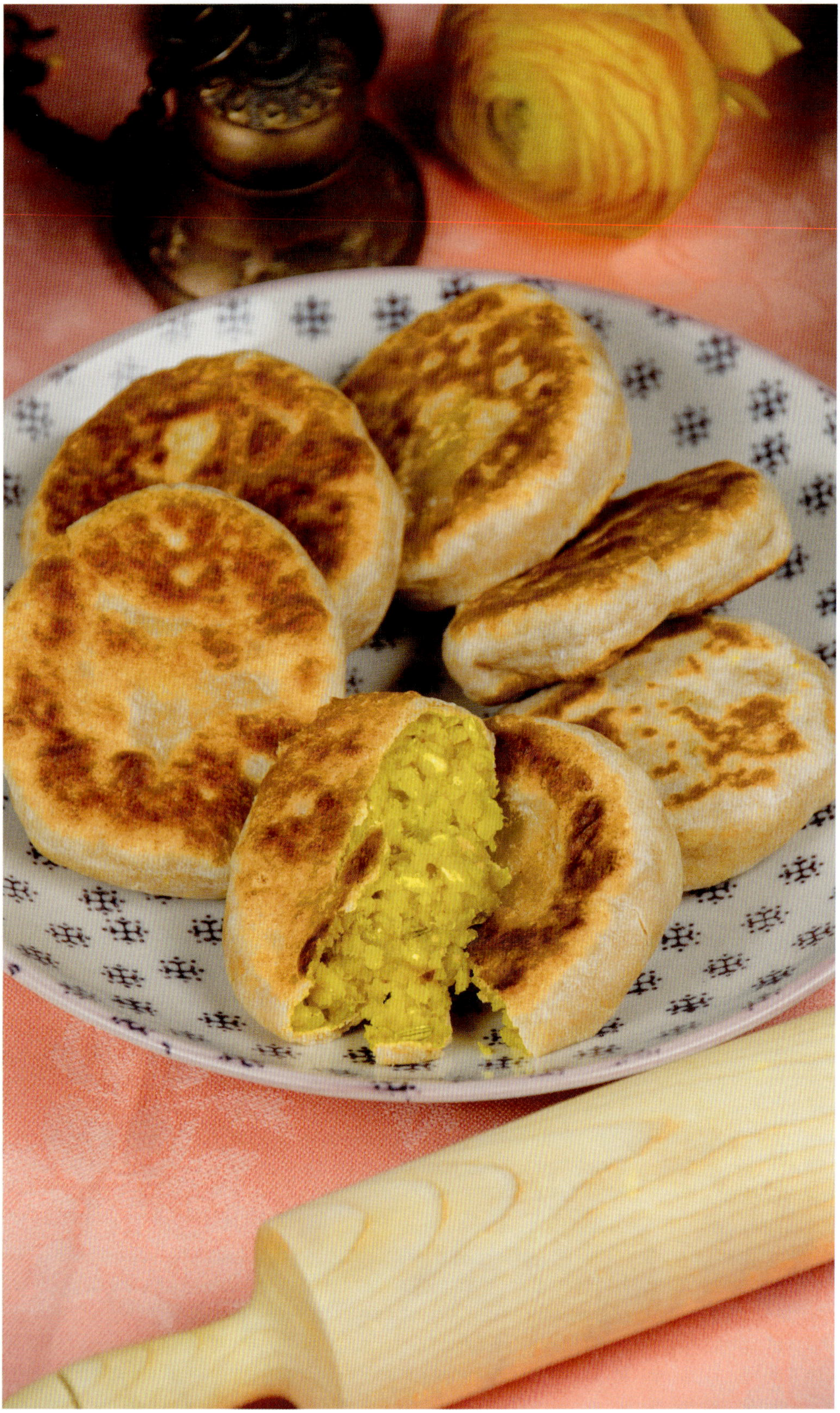

DAL KATCHORI – FLATBREAD FILLED WITH SPICY DAL
6-8 people

INGREDIENTS:

1,5 cup (200 g) whole-grain flour - wheat or spelt
⅔ cup (100 g) unbleached cake flour
80 g butter or coconut fat
1 tsp. salt - for the dough
½ tsp. baking powder
½ tsp. black pepper
½ cup (about 120-150 ml) water or as needed
100 g mung dal (soaked overnight)

½ tsp. salt for the filling
½ cumin seeds
½ tsp. fennel seeds
½ tsp. asafetida
½ tsp. turmeric
1 chili pod, seeded and finely chopped
1 tbsp. fresh coriander, finely chopped
oil for griddle frying

PREPARATION:

In a large bowl, mix both kinds of flour and crumble the butter into the flour with your fingers. Add the baking powder, salt and water and knead the dough on a floured work surface. The dough should be smooth and not sticky. Let the dough rest for 20 minutes, covered with a kitchen towel. Wash the mung dal and cook until soft in ½ L water (about 25 minutes). Drain well (if needed, you can rinse the dal with cold water and put it in a sieve to dry) and then put in a bowl. Fry the fennel and cumin over moderate heat until golden brown in a small frying pan and grind coarsely in a stone mortar.

Add the roasted spices, asafetida, turmeric, salt, chili and fresh coriander to the mung dal mix and mash a little. Divide the dough into 16 balls and roll in the shape of 10 cm patties. Take a patty in your left hand and place 1 tbsp. of filling in the middle. With your right hand, stick the edges together so that a ball is formed. Carefully press the ball flat between your palms. Heat up some oil in a pan (just enough to cover the bottom of the pan) and fry 4-5 of the filled katchoris at a time. The heat should be low because the katchoris take longer to cook (about 4-5 minutes per side).

Watch carefully and remove when they are golden brown. Serve immediately.

SAMOSAS
Filled Pastries

Anyone who has ever tried this triangular filled pastry will never want to do without it. Samosas are among the most popular Ayurvedic snacks: savory, delicious, perfect as a snack while hiking, picnics, during the workday, or as a whole meal in combination with salad and yogurt. My samosas are baked in the oven and not deep-fried as usual.

ALOO GOBI SAMOSA STUFFED DUMPLINGS WITH CAULIFLOWER AND POTATOES (BAKED IN THE OVEN)
6 people

INGREDIENTS:

1 cup (130 g) whole-grain flour
1 cup (150 g) unbleached cake flour
100 g butter or 2 tbsp. ghee or 2 big tbsp. virgin coconut oil
½ tsp. baking powder
1 tsp. salt - for the dough
2 tsp. sesame or flax seeds (optional)
about ½ cup (about 120-150 ml) water or as needed
500 g floury potatoes, peeled and cut into small pieces
1 small cauliflower, cut very small

100 g peas
1 tsp. turmeric
⅓ tsp. ground cinnamon
¼ tsp. ground cloves
½ tsp. asafetida
1 tsp. ground coriander
½ tsp. ajwain seeds, coarsely crushed
1 tbsp. fresh ginger, finely grated
½ lemon, squeezed
1 tsp. black salt - for the filling
1 tsp. ghee

PREPARATION:

In a bowl, combine flour, baking powder and salt and mix the butter into the flour with your fingertips. Add the sesame or flax seeds. Pour water slowly and only as much as needed. Knead the dough until smooth. Cover the dough with a kitchen towel and let it rest 15 minutes. Cook the potatoes, cauliflower and peas until tender in succession in the same cooking water. Drain well. Mash the potatoes in a bowl and then add the cauliflower and peas. Heat the ghee in a small pan and fry the spices over moderate heat: ajwain, coriander, asafetida, turmeric and ginger. Pour the toasted masala into the potato-cauliflower-peas mixture and add ground cinnamon, ground cloves, salt and lemon juice. Shape the dough into a snake and cut into 16 equal pieces. Form the pieces into small balls and, with a bit of flour, roll out in about 2 mm thin, circular patties. Place 1 tbsp. of filling on one-half of the flat cake, then fold over the other half and press the two layers of dough on the edge of the filling firmly together. Form the samosa edge by overlapping and folding piece by piece or simply squeezing with a fork. Heat up the oven to 180° C (356° F), place the samosas on a greased baking sheet and bake until golden brown 25-30 minutes. Brush the hot samosas with a little butter.

SPINACH POTATO SAMOSAS
6 people

INGREDIENTS:

1 cup (130 g) whole-grain flour
1 cup (150 g) unbleached cake flour
100 g butter or 2 tbsp. ghee or
2 big tbsp. virgin coconut oil
½ tsp. baking powder
1 tsp. salt - for the dough
2 tsp. sesame or flax seeds (optional)
½ cup (about 120-150 ml) water
700 g floury potatoes
700 g fresh spinach
1 tsp. turmeric
½ tsp. of asafetida

1 tsp. ground coriander
1 tsp. fenugreek seeds
1 tsp. ground cumin
1 tbsp. fresh ginger, finely grated
½ lemon, squeezed
1 tsp. salt - for the filling
2 chili pods, seeded and chopped
1 pinch of nutmeg
1 tsp. ghee
1 tsp. black salt - for the filling
1 tsp. ghee

PREPARATION:

In a bowl, combine flour, baking powder and salt and mix in the butter with your fingertips. Add the sesame or flax seeds and pour in water, as needed. Knead the dough until smooth. Cover the dough with a kitchen towel and let rest 15 minutes. Peel potatoes, chop coarsely and boil in water until soft. Drain well and then mash. Wash the spinach well, drain and chop coarsely. Steam the spinach in a very small amount of water until tender. Drain very well or press the water out with your hands, because spinach contains a lot of water and too much can open the pastry.

Heat up the ghee in a pan and quickly roast all the spices. Use always moderate heat when you assemble a masala (spice mix). Put the potatoes, spinach, spices, salt and lemon juice in a bowl and mix well. The filling should be room temperature. Shape the dough into a snake and cut into 16 equal pieces. Form the pieces into small balls and then roll out with a bit of flour into thin circular patties that about 2 mm. Place 1 big tbsp. of filling on one-half of the patty, and fold the other half over and squeeze together firmly. Form the samosa edge by overlapping and folding piece by piece or simply by squeezing with a fork.

Heat up the oven to 180° C (356° F), place the samosas on a greased baking sheet and bake until golden brown 25-30 minutes. Brush the hot samosas with butter or virgin coconut oil.

Snacks, Patties, Casseroles & Pilafs

161

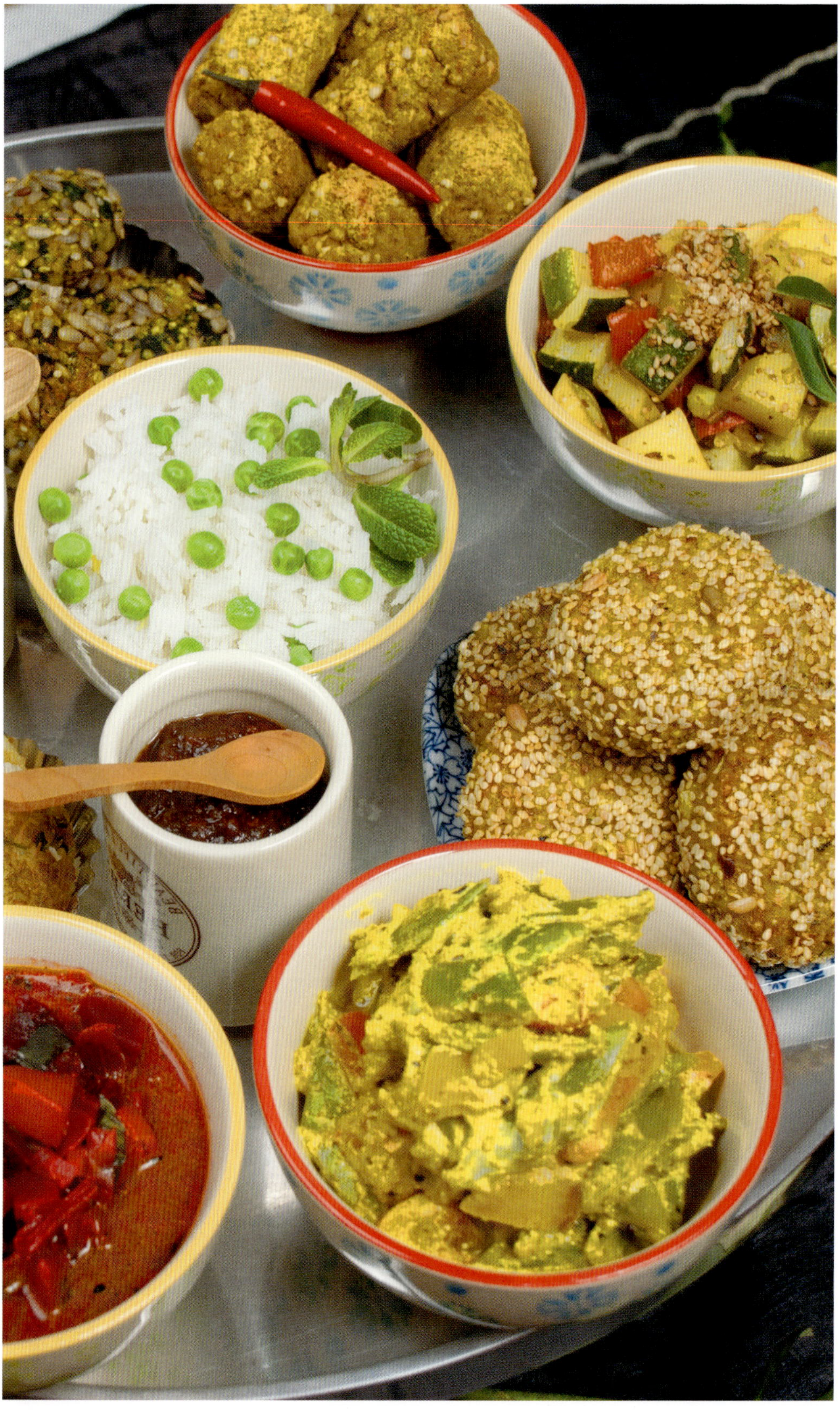

CEREAL GRAINS, POTATOES, CHICKPEAS
Snacks, patties, casseroles & pilafs – add a salad for a full meal

I depend upon casseroles, pilafs and patties made from grains, because grains are their most important component. Grain is our staple food. It not only contains carbohydrates, but also protein (up to 15%). The protein from grains is complete only when we have it in combination with legumes. That's why there are so many dishes where these two staple foods are eaten together. Whether it's dal with rice, beans with corn, lentils with dumplings, humus with pita bread, everywhere around the world, we can delve into the old traditions of food and the wonderful, nourishing and perfect mixture of nutrients. If we do not cook legumes with grains, we can optimize the protein by adding nuts and seeds. Also a dollop of organic Demeter yogurt or a handful of paneer (homemade cheese) in combination with grains can be used for the daily protein requirement. We distinguish between gluten-containing grains, like all wheat species, rye, barley and oats and gluten-free cereals such as corn, millet and rice. In addition, there are pseudo-grains like buckwheat, quinoa and amaranth.

ANCIENT WHEAT (not over-bred, organic) is a luxury grain, according to Ayurveda, very nourishing and tasty, because of its sweetness. In the Western world, we eat almost all of our dishes: bread, cakes and pasta from modern wheat, which has changed due to selective breeding and genetic modification. The excessive amount of processing and its large proportion of gluten in white flour cause digestive difficulties and various intolerances for many people. Wheat, in itself, is a great food, as long as one uses original wheat (e.g. from Demeter-certified sources) for cooking & baking. Convenient finished products such as couscous and bulgur are peeled, pre-cooked wheat. Spelt, emmer, einkorn and kamut are different types of original wheat grains. They do not contain much gluten and have not been changed so radically as modern wheat, therefore these original grains can be better tolerated. Grünkern is the immature spelt and is mostly used for patties.

OATS are a powerhouse of nutrients and remedies. They provide energy and help to maintain good health and vigor. Oats are not only processed as muesli, but they are delicious in energy balls, pies, soups and cookies. Oats are better tolerated than wheat because they do not contain as much gluten.

RYE is a robust crop and grows and thrives well, even under winter conditions. It's often planted after the summer harvest as a secondary crop. Rye contains less gluten than wheat and needs a leavening agent such as a sourdough starter to digest it properly.

BARLEY is also an ancient grain and as such is very resistant. Barley is known by many names: unhulled barley (naked barley) and hulled barley (pearl barley). Barley is not heavily over-bred like wheat and can be used for risotto (instead of rice), patties, casseroles, or soups. Also barley together with vegetables and chickpeas can make a delicious Tajine (Moroccan casserole). Best of all, barley porridge for breakfast, with apple-ginger compote, is a symphony for the stomach and intestines. Barley is also an effective natural remedy to extract excess water from the body. By drinking barley water regularly, water retention will be reduced.

MILLET is one of the oldest cereals and contains no gluten. It is a very versatile grain and can be prepared sweet as well as salty. Millet contains many minerals and is therefore good for teeth, bones, skin, hair and nails. Millet is very dry in the property and therefore an ideal food to help shed excess weight. Sweet porridge, casseroles with fruit, patties, pilafs and so on can be prepared with millet.

CORN, together with soy, is the most widely-modified plant in the world. Use only quality organic semolina, corn starch and corn flour. Otherwise, you can assume 100% that the grain is genetically-engineered. Corn is gluten-free and is great for casseroles, pizza dough and polenta. Even some cakes and bread are good with corn.

Just add some corn flour to the dough and enjoy a crispy-golden bread.

RICE feeds more people than any other grain. It is lighter than wheat and oats and more versatile than any other cereal. From rice, you can make pilafs, patties, casseroles, pancakes, simple side dishes or sweet puddings. Rice, as a staple, contains many essential amino acids. In combination with lentils, dairy products or nuts, rice provides the body with a complete source of protein. Basmati rice is the king of all rice varieties. It is most appreciated due to its aroma and fragrance. Thermic effect is cooling and ideal in summer as well as for pitta-types.

BUCKWHEAT is pseudo-grain, because it does not belong to edible grains like the real cereal grains. The buckwheat family is related to sorrel and rhubarb.
Buckwheat is also growing in Europe, but has disappeared from everyday life, it is called an "alternative grain". It is delicious when dry-roasted in the oven to 180° C for 15-20 minutes, which gives it wonderful nutty note and full-bodied taste. Buckwheat is my favorite cereal, because it is not a real grain. It can be cooked like rice (with much less water: 1 cup of buckwheat - 1.5 cups of water) and can be served with stir-fries, curries and stews as a side dish. Buckwheat is also good for making soups, pancakes (blinis) or added to nuggets.

QUINOA is an ancient Inca cereal and is related to the goosefoot family. This pseudo-grain contains, along with amaranth, the most protein and is a complete meal in itself. Quinoa can be used to prepare wonderful pilafs with vegetables and cashews, as well as an addition to soups or cooked salads.

AMARANTH is a pseudo-cereal and tastes nutty. Amaranth is usually popped and then added to cereals. The flour can be used as a delicious binding agent for soups and stews. Amaranth flour can also be added to cake dough, along with wheat or spelt flour to pep up the cake with valuable nutrients.

CHICKPEAS

SECRETS OF THE HAPPY LEGUME
Chickpeas are the kings of the legumes. So delicious and versatile in taste! They originally came from the south of Europe, but now they are grown in large quantities throughout the world. They have up to 20% protein and many minerals like potassium, magnesium and iron. From chickpeas come the tastiest dishes such as humus, salads, soups, stews and curries. Chickpea flour is made from peeled black chickpeas (chana dal) and is an indispensable ingredient for falafel patties, fritters and nuggets. Chickpea flour can also be used to make the most famous Ayurvedic sweet: Laddu.

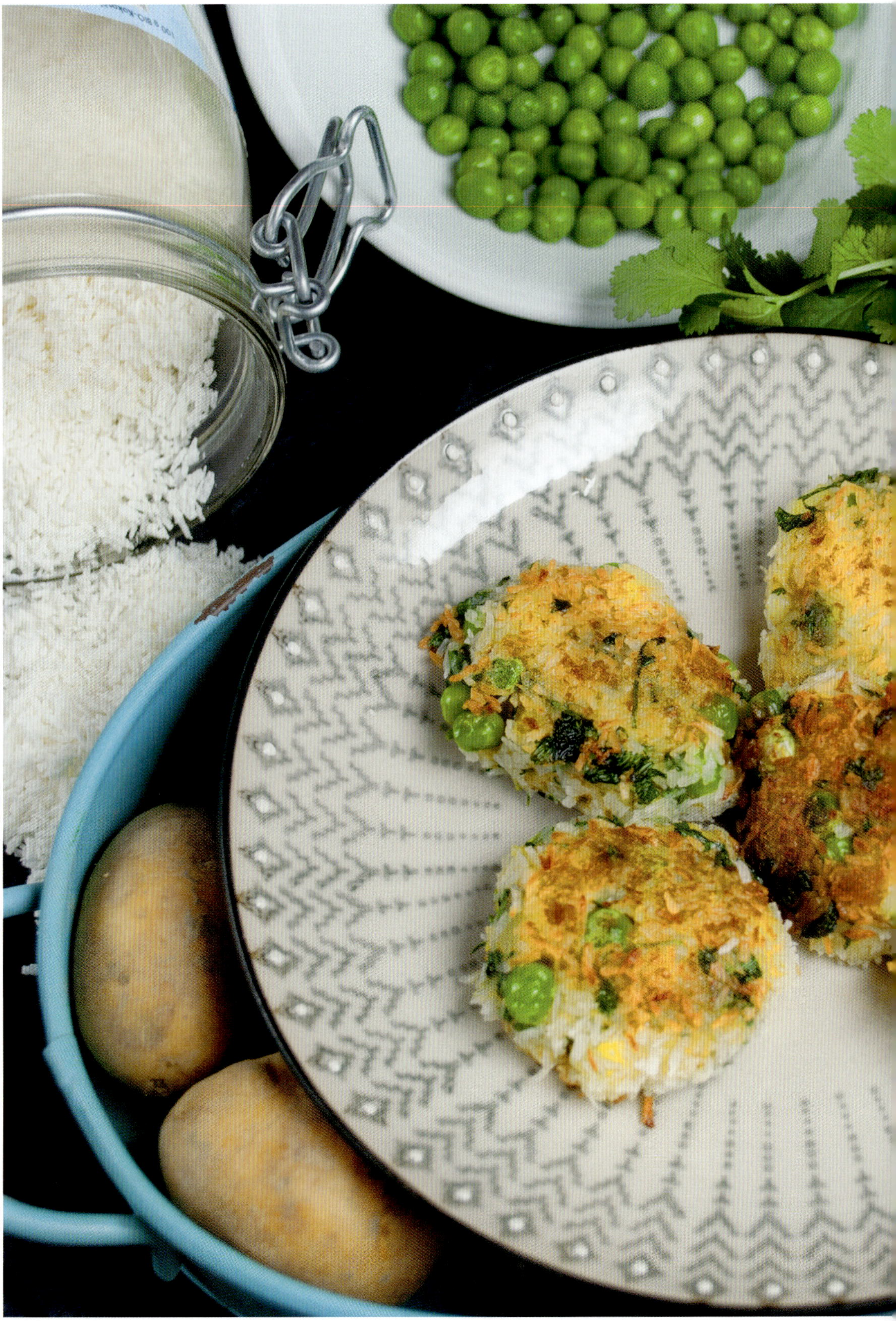

POTATO AND CORIANDER PATTIES IN COCONUT CRACKLING
6 people

INGREDIENTS:

1 kg waxy potatoes
100 g green peas (frozen peas can be used)
1 bunch fresh cilantro, parsley, or basil
1-2 tsp. cornstarch
½ tsp. asafetida
½ tsp. paprika
½ tsp. turmeric
½ lemon, squeezed
½ tsp. garam masala
1-½ tsp. salt
½ tsp. pepper
shredded coconut for rolling

PREPARATION:

Peel the potatoes, chop coarsely and cook until tender, drain well and mash. Cook the green peas and drain well. Mix potatoes and peas with all the spices and cornstarch and form patties. Roll it in some shredded coconut. Grease a heavy frying pan with ghee or some oil (just for the pan base). Fry the patties slowly over moderate heat and turn until both sides are golden brown and crispy.

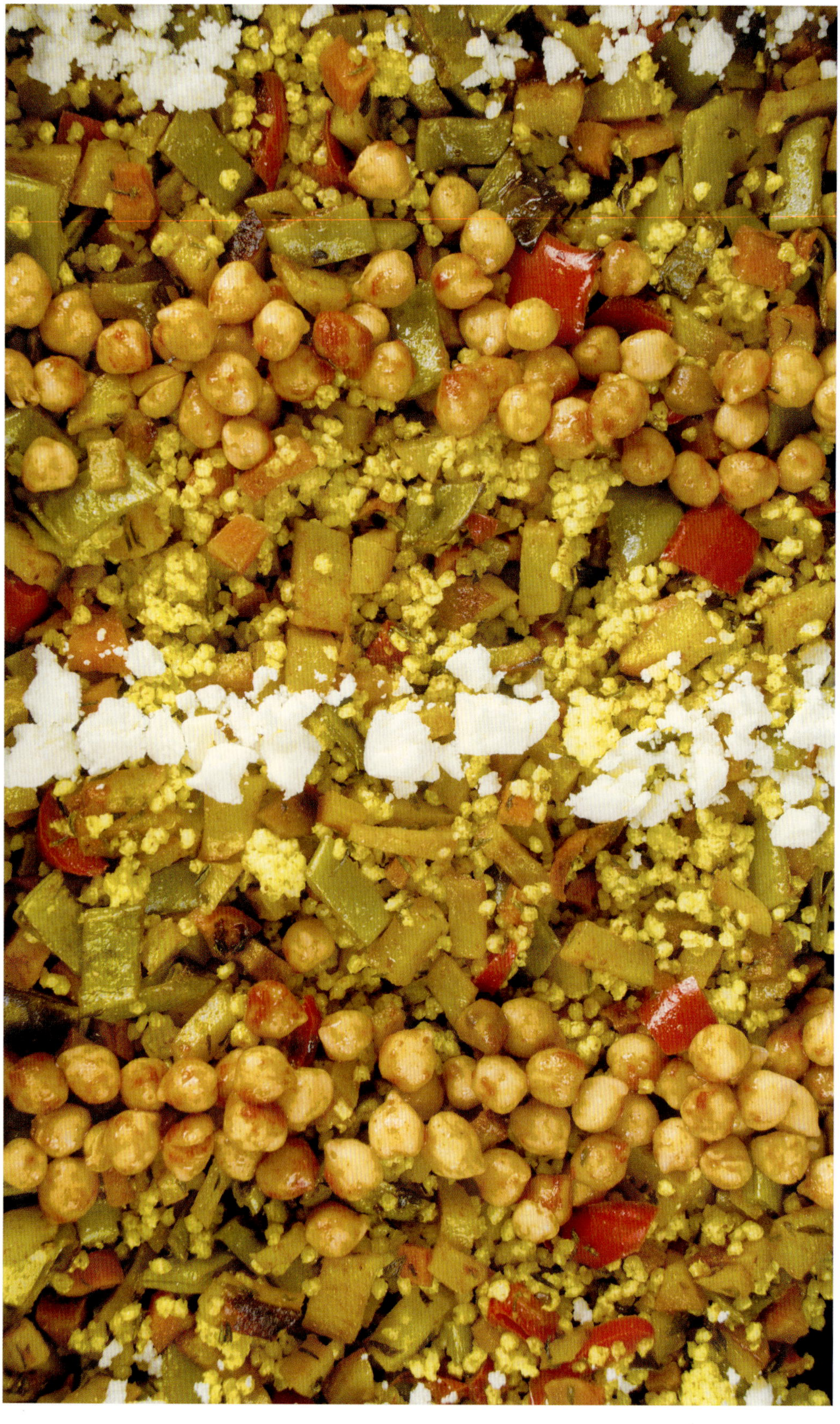

MILLET CHICKPEA PULAO WITH VEGETABLES
4 people

INGREDIENTS:

200 g (about 1,5 cup) millet
100 g cooked chickpeas
1 tsp. salt - for the pulao
3-4 potatoes
½ tsp. salt - for potatoes
1 red pepper
200 g green beans
100 g feta cheese, cut into small cubes
2 carrots
100 g cashews
2 tomatoes
½ tsp. of asafetida
1 tsp. turmeric
2 tbsp. fresh herbs to taste
½ tsp. sweet paprika powder
2 chili pods, finely chopped
1 tsp. salad herbs, dried
½ tsp. thyme or oregano, dried
1 lemon, squeezed
4-5 tbsp. olive oil

PREPARATION:

Wash millet and cook in plenty of water until the grains are cooked, but not falling apart (about 15-20 minutes). Rinse with cold water and drain. Peel, wash and dice the potatoes. Sprinkle with a little olive oil and salt and bake until golden brown in the oven at 220° C (428° F) for 30 minutes. Cut the green beans into 3 cm pieces and wash. Peel the carrots, wash and cut into sticks. Wash the peppers and cut into small cubes. Wash the tomatoes, remove seeds, and cut into small cubes. Steam the green beans and carrots quickly until they are al dente. Heat the olive oil in a wok and fry the cashews and pepper cubes in it, then add the asafetida, chili peppers, paprika and turmeric and fry for a few seconds. Now add the tomatoes, fresh herbs, thyme, salt, steamed vegetables and millet and mix well. Finally, add the baked potatoes, lemon, cooked chickpeas and feta cheese and stir gently. Sprinkle a little olive oil over the top.
Finished!

SIMPLE SWISS POTATO PATTIES "RÖSTI"
3-4 people

INGREDIENTS:

700 g potatoes
½ tsp. asafetida
10 cm piece of leek (cut into strips)
1 lemon, squeezed
1 tbsp. of chickpea flour
½ tsp. sweet paprika powder
1 tsp. salt
⅓ tsp. black pepper
sunflower oil – for griddle frying

PREPARATION:

Peel the potatoes and finely grate them. Immediately sprinkle with lemon juice so that the potatoes do not turn gray. Mix in all the other spices, leek strips and chickpea flour and stir well. Heat up sunflower oil in a heavy pan (just enough to cover the base of a pan) and, at the same time, form thin flat patties from the grated potatoes. Fry 3-4 patties in the pan slowly until golden brown. Patties that were shaped properly should not fall apart during cooking because potatoes contain a lot of starch, which acts as a binding agent.
   Serve hot.

CHICKPEA NUGGETS
3-4 people

INGREDIENTS:

2 cups (about 200 g) dry chickpeas soaked overnight
2 tbsp. fresh herbs (cilantro is the best)
½ cup (125 ml) buckwheat
1 tsp. sweet paprika powder
1 tsp. curry powder
½ tsp. coriander, ground
½ tsp. black pepper
1 tsp. salt
1 chili pod, seeded and chopped
½ lemon, squeezed
1 tbsp. bread crumbs or as needed to form the patties
virgin sesame oil for griddle frying

PREPARATION:

Cover the chickpeas in a saucepan or pot with water and cook about 1 ½-2 hours until they are soft. Stir often and, if necessary, pour in more water. Rinse with cold water and drain well. Cook the buckwheat in a cup of water until tender (about 12 minutes). In a food processor, mix all the ingredients and grind into a mass. If the mass is too soft, simply add a few breadcrumbs. Make flat patties and fry in a pan with a little sesame oil or bake for 20 minutes in oven at 180° C (356° F). Serve immediately.

GREEN SPELT MARJORAM PATTIES
6 people

INGREDIENTS:

2 cups (400 g) unripe spelt grain, soaked overnight (you can also use plain whole wheat grain or barley)
1 tsp. salt
2 tsp. marjoram, dried
1 tsp. sweet paprika powder
½ tsp. asafetida
½ tsp. turmeric
1 tsp. caraway seeds, crushed
1 tsp. black pepper
½ tsp. smoky salt (optional)
sunflower oil for griddle frying

PREPARATION:

In a pot, bring 2 l (about 6-8 cups) of water to a boil. Drain the green spelt and pour it into the boiling water. Cook for ½ hour without a lid. The unripe grains should be soft enough so that you can crush them between 2 fingers. Rinse the grains and drain well. Place in a food processor or mincer and grind coarsely. Place the mass in a bowl, add all the spices, and knead it into dough. Shape into flat patties and fry in a pan with a little ghee or sunflower oil until golden brown.

MILLET AND CARROT PATTIES
3-4 people

INGREDIENTS:

1.5 cup (200 g) millet
2 carrots, peeled and finely grated
2 tbsp. fresh cilantro or parsley, finely chopped
1 tsp. marjoram, dried
½ tsp. asafetida
½ tsp. turmeric
½ tsp. black pepper
50 g goat cheese, finely grated (optional)
50 g sunflower or pumpkin seeds, roasted and coarsely ground
1 tsp. salt

PREPARATION:

Wash millet, place in a pot with plenty of water and bring to a boil. Cook until you can mash the grains between 2 fingers (about 15 minutes). Rinse with cold water and drain well. In a saucepan, heat up 1 tsp. ghee and fry the carrots in it for 2 minutes at low heat, and then add the asafetida, turmeric, pepper, coriander, marjoram and sunflower seeds and fry for another minute. Now take the pan off the heat, add the millet, fresh coriander, salt, and goat cheese and mash everything well. It should result in a sticky mass. From the mass, press into compact, flat patties. Fry in a pan with very little oil until golden brown. Millet is very rich in minerals. The sunflower seeds and the goat cheese supply the body with protein.

Note: Add some cooked, well drained spinach to the Millet-Patties, you will get perfect combination!

CARROT AND COCONUT CHICKPEA VADA (FRIED PATTIES)
6-8 people

INGREDIENTS:

700 g carrots
3 tbsp. grated coconut
100 g chickpea flour
½ tsp. baking powder
1 tsp. salt
1 tsp. garam masala
1 tsp. turmeric
½ tsp. asafetida
1 tbsp. fresh herbs
½ tsp. ground coriander
sunflower oil for frying

PREPARATION:

Peel and wash the carrots. Shred the carrots fine in a food processor. In a bowl, mix all the spices with the shredded carrots, chickpea flour, coconut, salt and baking powder to form a moist dough. From the mass, form small flat patties (the softer the patties are, the more succulent they will be). Heat 700 ml sunflower oil in a heavy pan and fry the patties until golden brown.

CAULIFLOWER KOFTA "GOBI KOFTA"
(FRIED BALLS FROM CAULIFLOWER AND CHICKPEA FLOUR)
6 people

INGREDIENTS:

1 medium cauliflower, cut into small pieces
100 g chickpea flour
1 tbsp. fresh coriander or parsley, finely chopped
½ tsp. baking powder
1 tsp. salt
1 tsp. fresh ginger, finely grated
½ tsp. ground cinnamon
1 tsp. ground coriander
⅓ tsp. ground cumin
⅓ tsp. asafetida
1 tsp. turmeric
⅓ tsp. black pepper
sunflower oil for frying

PREPARATION:

Finely grind cauliflower in a food processor. Mix in one bowl: chickpea flour, all spices, salt, baking powder, fresh herbs, and crushed cauliflower. Mix and knead into a moist mass. Heat up 700 ml sunflower oil and drop in tablespoon-sized balls into the hot oil. The balls will fall to the bottom. Let the balls fry over moderate heat for about 1-2 minutes. They need enough time to become firm. After a few minutes, you can take the balls with a slotted spoon and bring them up gently to the surface. Let them cook on the surface for another 2-3 minutes. The finished balls should have a beautiful golden brown color. Remove with a sieve and drain well on a paper towel. You will get 20-25 kofta balls..

PUDLA - PATTIES MADE WITH CHICKPEA FLOUR AND VEGETABLES
4-6 people

INGREDIENTS:

1 cup (70-100 g) chickpea flour
1 red pepper, grated
1 carrot, peeled and grated
1 zucchini (courgette), grated
1 slice of Hokkaido pumpkin, grated
1 chili, finely chopped
1 tbsp. parsley, finely chopped
½ tsp. asafetida
½ tsp. turmeric
½ tsp. ground coriander
½ tsp. nigella seeds (kalonji)
½ tsp. black pepper
1 tsp. salt
½ tsp. baking powder
sesame or sunflower oil for griddle frying

PREPARATION:

Add the chickpea flour, all spices, baking powder and salt to a large bowl. Pour in the grated vegetables and stir well with a big spoon. This should result in a sticky mass. You may need to add some water (just 2-3 tbsp.). Heat some oil in a pan (just to cover the base) and drop 1 tablespoon of the sticky mass, one by one, in the pan. There should be 5-6 pancakes in one batch in a pan. It is important to slowly cook the pancakes on both sides. They should be crisp and golden brown. Continue in this way, adding new oil on the base for each new batch of pancakes. Serve hot.

UPPMA (HEARTY VEGETABLE SPELT SEMOLINA STEW) SOUTH INDIAN SPECIALITY
6 people

INGREDIENTS:

100 g butter or 2 tbsp. of ghee or 2 tbsp. virgin coconut fat
1.5 cups (250 g) spelt or wheat semolina
1.5 cups (150 g) green beans, chopped
2 carrots, peeled and cut into sticks
1 red or green bell pepper, cut into small pieces
½ broccoli or ¼ white cabbage, finely chopped
2 tbsp. tomato paste
1 tbsp. fresh ginger, grated
1 chili, finely chopped
1 tsp. fenugreek powder
1 tsp. turmeric
1 tsp. coriander
½ tsp. asafetida
1 tsp. black mustard seeds
½ tsp. cumin seeds
1 tsp. ghee for masala
1-2 tsp. salt
3 cups (750 ml) water

PREPARATION:

Heat up the ghee in a saucepan and pour in the black mustard seeds. Cover and wait until the mustard seeds no longer jump. Turn the heat down and add the cumin seeds and roast until brown. Add the well-drained vegetables (except the broccoli) and fry briefly. Add the chili, fenugreek, asafetida, turmeric, coriander and ginger and fry briefly. Pour in the water. Cover and simmer for about 10 minutes. Add the broccoli, tomato paste and salt and simmer for another 5 minutes. In a skillet, melt butter and add the semolina. Roast the semolina about 10 minutes over moderate heat until the semolina has a fine golden-brown color. Add the semolina to the hot vegetable soup, being careful of the steam! Immediately use a whisk to stir the dish and avoid semolina lumps. Cook for 3 more minutes to let thicken. Remove from the heat and serve immediately.

AYURVEDIC LASAGNA WITH EGGPLANT, ZUCCHINI AND ALMOND BÉCHAMEL
6-8 people

INGREDIENTS:

200 g lasagna sheets - from rice, corn, durum wheat or spelt semolina, egg-free
½ cup or 4-5 tbsp. almond butter
3 cups (750 ml) water
½ tsp. of nutmeg powder
6 tbsp. olive oil
4 tbsp. unbleached white flour
1,5 tsp. salt for the Béchamel sauce
2 eggplants (aubergines)
2 zucchini (courgettes)
oil for frying
2 fennel bulbs

200 g feta cheese
1 cup (250 ml) of tomato juice
½ tsp. asafetida
1 tsp. turmeric
1 tsp. raw cane sugar
1 tsp. ground coriander
2 tsp. basil, dried
½ tsp. oregano, dried
½ tsp. thyme, dried
1 tsp. sweet paprika powder
½ tsp. caraway, ground
½ tsp. salt for tomato sauce

PREPARATION:

Heat the olive oil in a pan, add the flour and stir-fry 2 minutes over moderate heat. Add water, almond butter, nutmeg and salt and bring to a boil, stirring constantly. This should make a fairly thick sauce. Wash, dry and slice eggplants (aubergines) and zucchini (courgettes). Fry on both sides quickly in the pan with a little ghee or oil and drain on a paper towel. Add a little salt. Wash the fennel and chop coarsely. Steam briefly in a little water and add a little salt.

   Divide the eggplant, zucchini, and fennel mix into 2 equal parts. Cut feta cheese into thin slices or cubes. In a saucepan, heat up 1-2 tbsp. of olive oil and fry the spices briefly. Add the tomato juice, salt, and sugar and bring to a boil. Put aside. Grease a deep baking dish with olive oil, and then add a ladle of béchamel sauce. For the first layer, place the uncooked lasagna noodles on the bottom, and then the first layer of vegetables, then the feta cheese, and add 1-2 ladles of tomato sauce evenly on top. For the second layer, place the lasagna noodles, vegetables, cheese, and tomato sauce. Finally, add one more layer of lasagna noodles and pour over the rest of the Béchamel sauce.

   Cover the casserole with baking paper and bake in preheated oven at 200° C (392° F) for 40 minutes. For the last 10 minutes, you can uncover the lasagna, so it gets a nice golden brown color.

IDLI - SPICY DAL CEREAL DUMPLINGS SOUTH INDIAN SPECIALITY
6 people

INGREDIENTS:

1 cup (250 ml) white semolina, wheat or corn
1 tbsp. urad or mung dal, soaked at least 2 hours
1 cup (250 ml) yogurt
⅔ cup (130 ml) water or as needed
½ tsp. baking powder
1 tsp. salt
½ tsp. turmeric
⅓ tsp. black pepper
1 chili, finely chopped
1 tbsp. black mustard seeds
50 g cashews
2 tsp. ghee

PREPARATION:

For this dish, you will need a pot with a strainer made of stainless steel or an original South Indian idli pot with many small idli molds. This can be purchased in an Indian shop or ordered online. It is worth it. Idlis are an ideal food for vegetarians, as they provide an optimal combination of protein and carbohydrates. You can take idlis to work or on a trip instead of a sandwich. Drain the soaked dal and grind with the cashews in a food processor. Heat up the ghee in a small pot or a pan and pour in the mustard seeds. Cover the pot and wait until the mustard seeds no longer jump. Pour in the ground dal and cashew with chopped chili and fry until golden brown. Put aside. In a glass bowl, pour in the semolina, salt, pepper, turmeric and baking powder. Add the yogurt and the water and stir until smooth. Pour in the roasted spice-dal-cashew mixture and stir briefly and firmly. Pour the sticky mass into a greased steamer insert and spread evenly. Pour some water into the pot (so that base of the pot has 2 cm of water), place the steamer insert with the idli dough, and cover. Simmer for about 15-20 minutes (12 minutes with an original idli pot) until the mass has risen nicely. Remove the steamer insert, cut into pieces and serve immediately. They can be eaten on the next day as well, as they remain juicy and fresh. You can combine this with a good coconut-yogurt chutney or a vegetable dish.

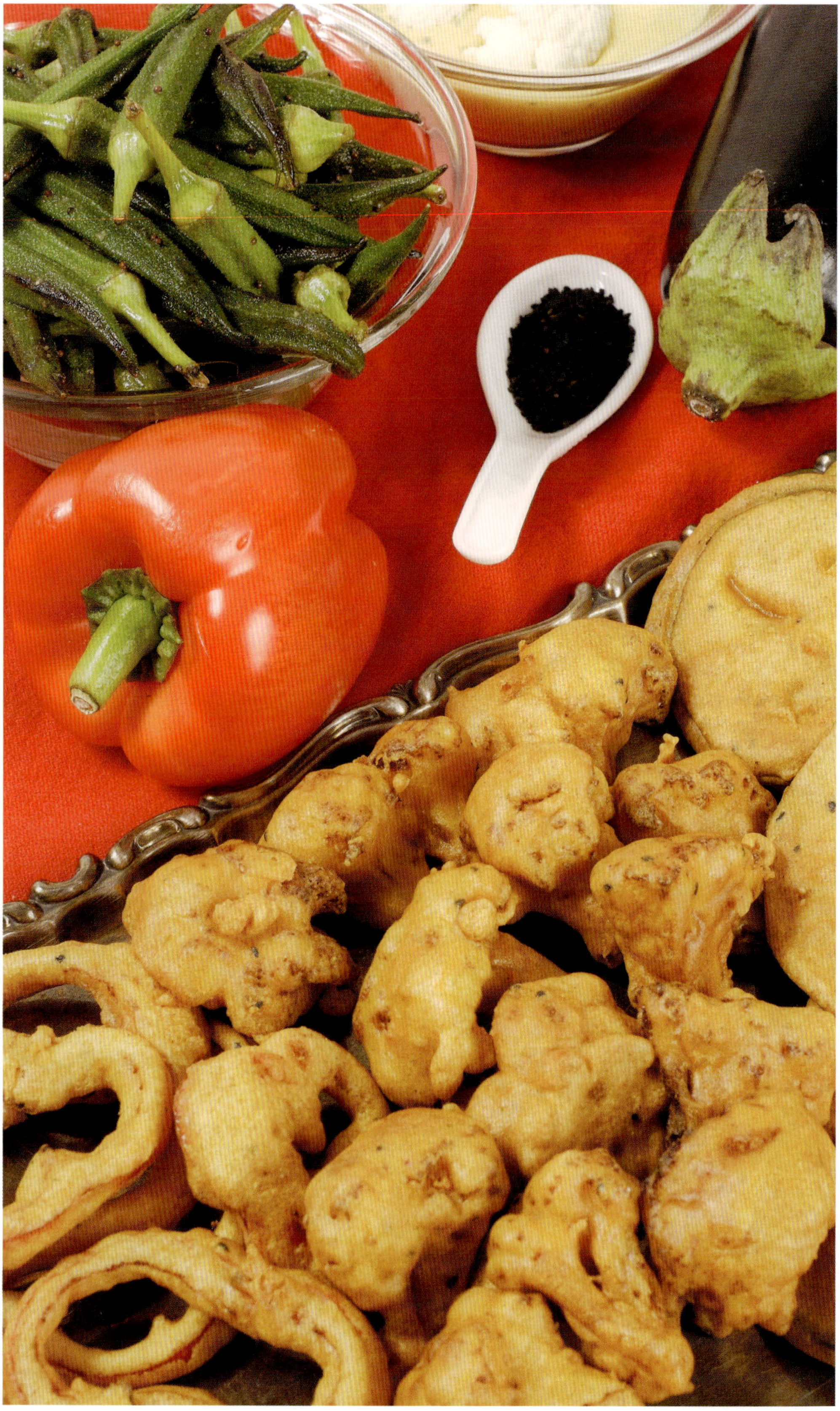

"PAKORA" FRIED VEGETABLES IN CHICKPEA DOUGH
6-8 people

INGREDIENTS:

1.5 cup (200) g chickpea flour
1 tsp. nigella seeds (kalonji or black cumin)
½ tsp. cinnamon powder
1 pinch of chili powder
1 tsp. ground coriander
1 tsp. turmeric
½ tsp. asafetida
1-½ tsp. salt
1 pinch of baking soda
1.3 cup (300 ml) of water
700 ml sunflower oil for frying
1 cauliflower, washed and cut into small florets
1 eggplant, washed and cut into thick slices (0.5 cm thick)

PREPARATION:

Pour the chickpea flour into a large bowl and mix in the spices, salt and baking soda. Pour in cold water and beat with a whisk until the dough is smooth enough and thick enough to coat the vegetables. Heat up the sunflower oil. It's hot enough when a drop of dough rises immediately to the surface while hissing. Add a handful of vegetables into the batter and stir until they are completely covered. Take the coated vegetables out one by one and place quickly in the hot oil. Let them fry for a few minutes until they are golden brown. Remove and drain well.

CABBAGE KOFTA (DEEP-FRIED BALLS)
6-8 people

INGREDIENTS:

½ head of white or red cabbage, finely chopped
about 100 g (1 cup) chickpea flour
⅓ tsp. baking powder
1 tsp. salt
1 chili pod, finely chopped
1 tbsp. fresh herbs
1 tsp. ajwain seeds
1 tsp. ground coriander
½ tsp. ground cumin
¼ tsp. nutmeg powder
½ tsp. asafetida
1 tsp. turmeric

PREPARATION:

Grind the cabbage finely in a food processor. Place the grated cabbage in a bowl, add the herbs, spices, salt, baking powder and chickpea flour and mix well. There should be a wet, sticky mass formed. Heat up 700 ml sunflower oil for frying. Form small balls (about the size of a teaspoon) and fry in oil until golden brown. The balls will fall to the bottom. Let them cook for about 1-2 minutes. During this time, leave the balls on the bottom (do not stir or try to move them). They need enough time to become firm. After a few minutes, you can carefully pick up with a spatula or spoon and move them to the surface of the oil. Let them fry another 2-3 minutes. Carefully remove with a strainer and drain well on a paper towel.

Chutneys

9.

CHUTNEYS
Fruity spicy sauces

Chutneys are a mix of fruit, spices and raw sugar and should be on the menu daily. They are the perfect accompaniment to any main course, as they contain all six tastes and taste refreshingly fruity. Chutneys go very nicely with snacks or savories. Each entree benefits by adding 1-2 tsp. of chutney to taste. Apples, peaches and plums are particularly suitable for chutneys, but almost any fruit can be used. The secret of a good chutney is the right balance of ginger and chili. It is important to use a lot of fresh ginger and a moderate amount of chili. It is practical to prepare chutneys one day in advance, as they can be refrigerated.

APPLE AND GINGER CHUTNEY
6 people

INGREDIENTS:

1 kg of apples (4-5 apples)
1 tsp. ghee or 1 tbsp. of oil
1 tbsp. ginger, freshly grated
½ tsp. cinnamon powder
1 tsp. anise seeds
1 pinch ground cloves
½ tsp. turmeric
1 tbsp. raw cane sugar
1 pinch of salt

PREPARATION:

Wash the apples, peel, remove the seeds and cut into small pieces. Heat the ghee in a saucepan and quickly fry the anise seed. Then add the apples and the remaining spices. Fry everything for a few seconds. Then simmer the chutney in 4 tbsp. (50 ml) of water for 5 minutes with the lid on. Remove the lid and simmer for an additional 10 minutes until most of the water is evaporated. Finally, add the sugar and a pinch of salt and simmer for 2 minutes.

CARAMEL BANANA ALMOND CHUTNEY
6-8 people

INGREDIENTS:

3-4 pieces firm bananas, cut into thick slices of 2 cm
4 tbsp. raw cane sugar
1 tsp. cinnamon
⅓ tsp. chili powder
50 g almonds, whole and peeled
½ cup (125) ml of apple juice

PREPARATION:

In a saucepan, caramelize the sugar without stirring. Dilute the sugar with apple juice and cover the pot immediately. Watch out for the steam! Let the chutney simmer, until the sugar has completely dissolved.

Finally, add the chili, banana, cinnamon and almonds and cook for 2 minutes more.

MANGO MINT CHUTNEY
4 people

INGREDIENTS:

2 mangoes, peeled and cut into cubes
10 mint leaves, ground in a mortar
½ tsp. anise seeds
1 tbsp. fresh ginger, finely grated
1 pinch of salt
1 chili, finely chopped
½ lemon, squeezed
1 tbsp. raw cane sugar
1 tbsp. sesame oil
2 tbsp. water

PREPARATION:

In a saucepan, heat the sesame oil and fry the anise, ginger and chili over moderate heat. Add the mango and water and simmer covered for 5-7 minutes. Remove the lid, add sugar, lemon juice and salt and simmer another 5 minutes.

Finally, add the fresh ground mint, take the chutney from the heat and let it rest for 10 minutes.

APRICOT CHUTNEY
4-6 people

INGREDIENTS:

8 apricots, washed and quartered
½ tsp. nigella seeds (kalonji or black cumin seeds)
1 tbsp. fresh ginger, finely grated
1 chili, finely chopped
2 tbsp. raw cane sugar
1 pinch of salt
1 tablespoon sesame oil
2 tbsp. water

PREPARATION:

In a saucepan, heat the sesame oil and fry the nigella seeds for a few minutes. Then add the chili and ginger and continue to fry. Add the apricots, 2 tbsp. of water and simmer for 5 minutes, with the lid on. Remove the lid, add the sugar and salt and simmer for 3-4 minutes.

PLUM CHUTNEY
4-6 people

INGREDIENTS:

½ kg plums
1 tsp. ground coriander
1 tsp. anise seeds
½ tsp. cardamom, crushed
1 tablespoon shredded coconut
1 tbsp. fresh ginger, grated
2 tablespoon sesame oil
3 tbsp. raw cane sugar
2 chilies, chopped
3-4 tbsp. water
1 pinch of salt

PREPARATION:

Wash the plums, remove seeds, and cut into quarters. In a saucepan, heat the sesame oil and fry the anise seeds quickly. Add the coriander powder, chilies, and ginger and continue to fry for a few seconds. Add in the plum, cardamom, and coconut and stir well. Pour in the water, cover, and simmer about 5 minutes. Stir occasionally. Remove the cover, add sugar and salt and simmer another 10 minutes.

PEACH OR NECTARINE CHUTNEY
4-6 people

INGREDIENTS:

3 peaches or nectarines, washed and quartered
½ tsp. anise seeds
½ tsp. nigella seeds (kalonji seeds or black cumin seeds)
1 tsp. fresh ginger, finely grated
1 chili, finely chopped
1 pinch ground cloves
2 tbsp. raw sugar
1 tablespoon sesame oil
3 tbsp. water
1 pinch of salt

PREPARATION:

Heat up the sesame oil in a saucepan and fry the nigella seeds and anise for a few seconds. Add the ginger, chili, and cloves and continue to fry. Add the peaches, fry a little, and then pour in 3 tbsp. of water. Cover the chutney and simmer 5 minutes. Once the peaches have become soft, add the sugar and salt and simmer for another 3-4 minutes without a lid.

COCONUT YOGHURT DAL CHUTNEY
6-8 people

INGREDIENTS:

1 cup (250 ml) natural yogurt
½ cup (125 ml) of water
6 tbsp. shredded coconut
1 tablespoon urad dal, peeled and split
⅓ tsp. asafetida
1 tsp. black mustard seeds
2 chilies, finely chopped
2 tbsp. fresh cilantro or parsley, finely chopped
1 tsp. salt
10 fresh curry leaves (optional)
2 tablespoon sesame oil

PREPARATION:

Heat sesame oil in a small pan, add the mustard seeds and cover immediately. When the mustard seeds no longer jump, remove the lid and add in the urad dal. Roast slowly until golden brown. Add the asafetida, chili, and curry leaves and fry briefly. Remove the pan from the stove.

In a bowl, mix together the yogurt, coconut, water, fresh herbs and salt. Then add the roasted spices and dal and mix well. Refrigerate the chutney.

Salads & Raitas

10.

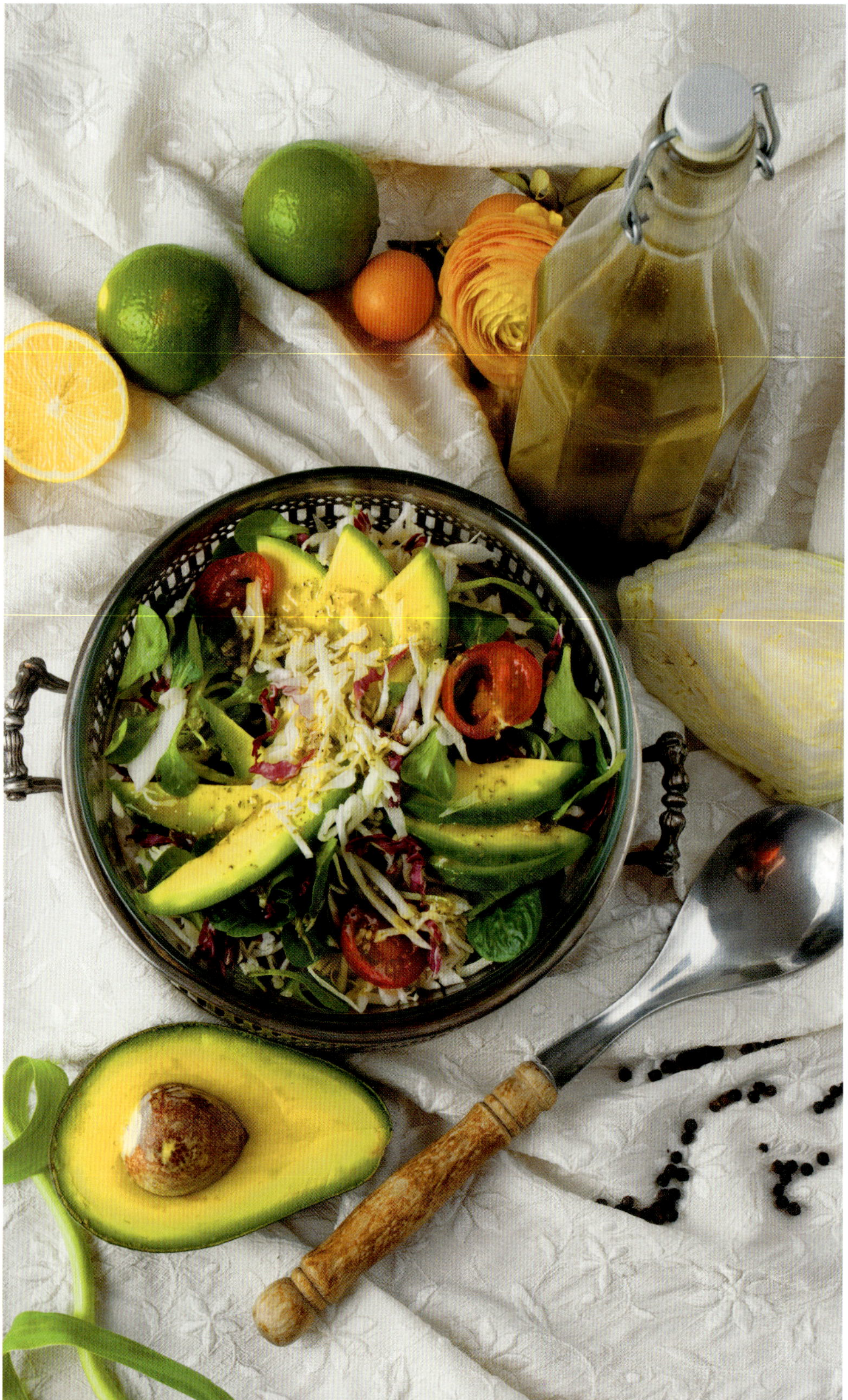

SALADS AND RAITAS
Raw vegetables for lunch

Salads are refreshing and light and should be eaten only at noon because they can be difficult to digest. Raitas are traditional relishes, which are prepared with raw or cooked vegetables and yogurt. Raitas are more filling, richer and spicier than an ordinary leafy salad. They enhance the taste of the main course and help digestion. A salad can be made richer, or can even become the main course, by adding a few noodles, avocado, tofu or croutons. Such salads are recommended especially during the heat of summer, because they are refreshing and easy to make and are still satisfying and nourishing. During the cold season, it is preferable to eat warm or boiled vegetables, cooked and flavoured with sweet and sour salad dressing.

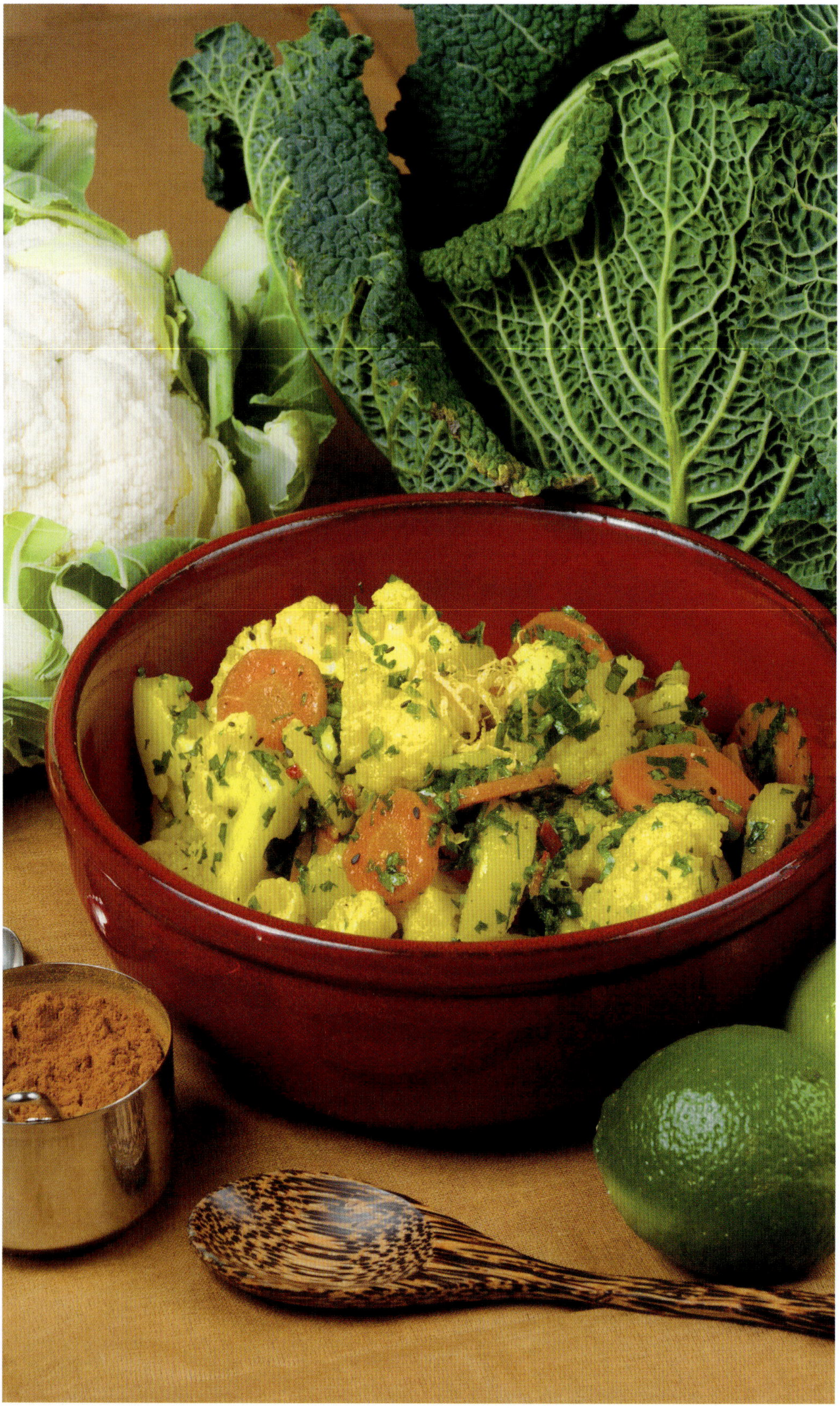

WARM VEGETABLE SALAD
4-6 people

INGREDIENTS:

½ cauliflower, cut into florets
3 potatoes, peeled and diced
2 carrots, peeled and cut into sticks
½ red bell pepper, cut into strips
3-4 tbsp. olive oil
½ lemon, squeezed
fresh herbs - best basil or parsley finely chopped
½ tsp. turmeric (optional)
½ tsp. black pepper
2-3 tbsp. sunflower seeds or pumpkin seeds, roasted

PREPARATION:

In a saucepan, bring 4 cups (1 l) of water to a boil and add the carrots and potatoes. Simmer for about 10 minutes. Add the cauliflower and red pepper and simmer for another 5 minutes. Add some turmeric powder in cookingwater to get a beautiful yellow cauliflower. Carefully pour off the water (you can save it for soup) and add the olive oil, lemon juice, fresh herbs, turmeric, pepper and seeds. Cook and stir gently. Finished!

This vegetable salad is an ideal accompaniment to fried vegetarian patties, polenta slices or simply with a piece of bread and a dollop of yogurt. You can also use green beans, broccoli, sweet potatoes, turnips, or cabbage. It is important that you always include a few potatoes so that it is filling.

SUMMER RICE SALAD WITH KALAMATA OLIVES, FETA CHEESE, AND VEGETABLES
4 people

INGREDIENTS:

1 cup (250) ml Arborio or Italian short-grain rice
1.9 cup (490 ml) water
1 tsp. ghee
1 red pepper, diced
1 zucchini, diced
1 carrot, diced
2 sheets chard, cut into strips
⅓ tsp. salt, for the vegetables

2 tbsp. olive oil
10-15 Kalamata olives, pitted and sliced
100 g feta cheese, cut into small cubes
10 leaves fresh basil, cut into thin strips
½ tsp. black pepper
1 tsp. salt – for the rice
½ tsp. asafetida
½ tsp. paprika
½ tsp. oregano
2 tomatoes, peeled, seeded and chopped
1 lemon, squeezed

PREPARATION:

In a saucepan, heat the ghee, add rice and sauté 1 minute. When the rice has become glassy, add the asafetida and fry briefly. Pour in the water, add salt, stir gently, cover and simmer for about 12-15 minutes over low heat. Heat 1 tbsp. sunflower oil in a wok and fry the chopped vegetables about 3-4 minutes, so that they are still firm to the bite (al dente). Add the salt, pepper, oregano, paprika, tomatoes and basil. Mix the vegetables, feta cheese, olives and lemon juice gently into the cooked rice.

    This dish can be enjoyed hot or cold.

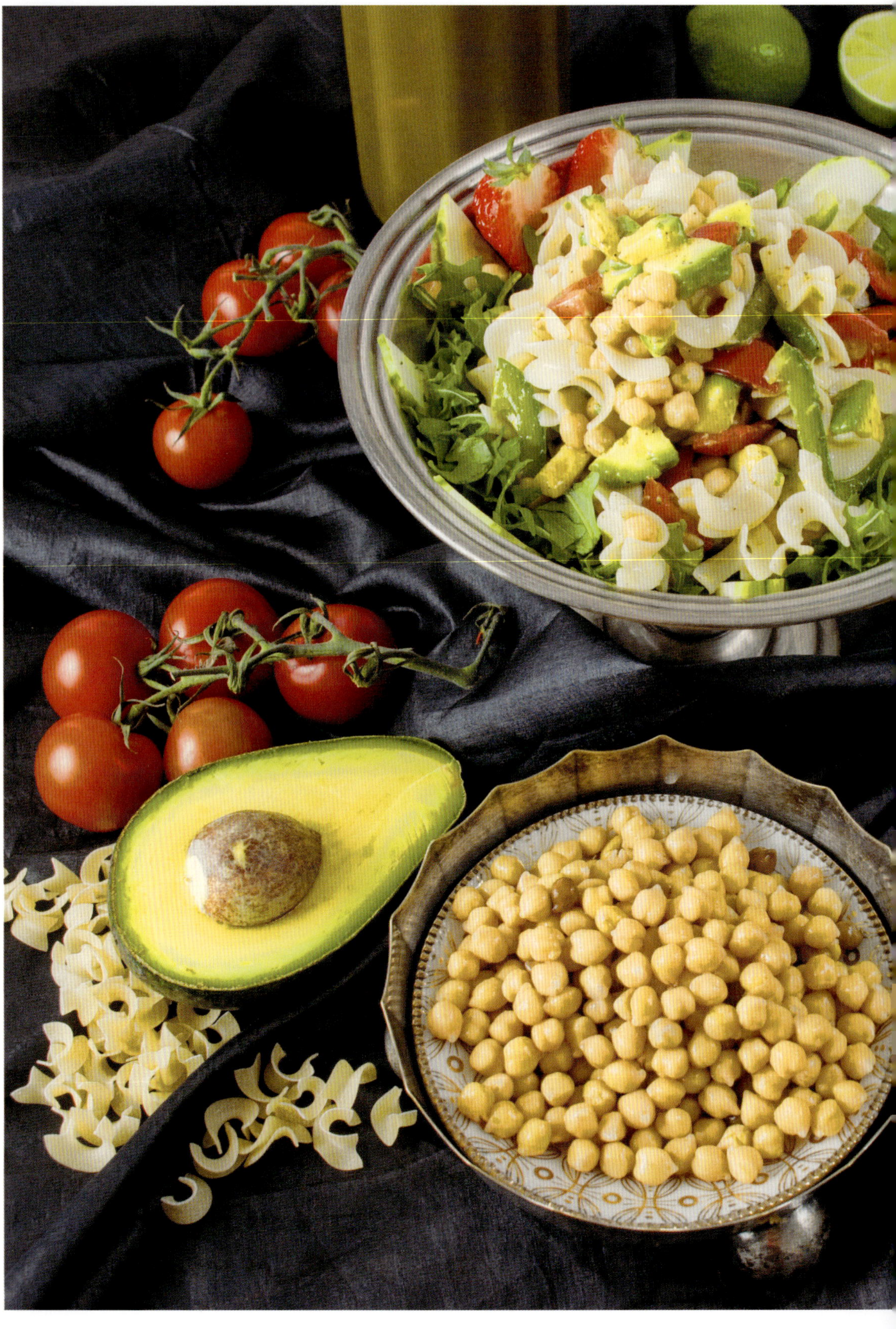

NOODLE AVOCADO CHICKPEA SALAD
4-6 people

INGREDIENTS:

100 g penne, farfalle or spirals – egg-free
1 avocado
1 cup (100 g) cooked chickpeas
2 tomatoes
½ red pepper
1 lemon, squeezed
4 tbsp. olive oil
10 fresh basil leaves, thinly sliced
1 tsp. salt
½ tsp. sugar
½ tsp. black pepper
½ tsp. sweet paprika powder

PREPARATION:

Soak the chickpeas overnight. The next day, cook the chickpeas for 1-½ hours in plenty of water. Rinse with cold water and drain well. Cook the pasta al dente and drain well. Wash the tomatoes, peppers and avocado and cut into small cubes. Immediately sprinkle with lemon juice, so the avocado does not become black.

Combine all the ingredients together and gently stir. Serve immediately.

WALDORF SALAD
2 people

INGREDIENTS:

1 apple
¼ celeriac, peeled
2 carrots
1 handful of nuts - walnuts, cashews or peeled, roasted almonds

DRESSING:

2 tbsp. olive oil
½ lemon, squeezed
5 tbsp. (50 ml) unfiltered apple juice
1 tsp. mustard (paste)
1 tsp. salad herbs
½ tsp. salt
pinch of black pepper

PREPARATION:

Peel and grate the apple, celery, and carrots. Mix the dressing well and pour over the salad. Finished!

ARUGULA TOFU AND TOMATO SALAD
3 people

INGREDIENTS:

100 g arugula
50 g radicchio
100 g tofu, natural or smoked, diced
2 tomatoes
2 tbsp. balsamic vinegar
1 tbsp. soy sauce
2 tbsp. virgin sunflower oil
50 ml apple juice, unfiltered
½ tsp. mustard (paste)
½ tsp. black salt (kala namak)
½ tsp. salad herbs
1 pinch black pepper
½ tsp. raw sugar
2 tbsp. sesame oil, cold-pressed

PREPARATION:

Heat 2 tbsp. sesame oil in a pan and fry the tofu cubes until golden brown. Add 1 tbsp. soy sauce and deglaze. Let cool.

Wash the arugula and radicchio and cut into strips. Wash the tomatoes and cut into cubes. To make the dressing, combine mustard, balsamic vinegar, sunflower oil, salt, salad herbs, apple juice, raw sugar and pepper. Stir together with a whisk.

Place the radicchio, arugula, tomatoes and tofu mix in a salad bowl, pour over the dressing and mix well. Serve immediately.

YOUNG CABBAGE & LAMB'S LETTUCE SALAD WITH AVOCADO
4 people

INGREDIENTS:

½ young cabbage
1 avocado
1 carrot
100 g lamb's lettuce or arugula
2 tbsp. sunflower seeds, roasted
½ lemon, squeezed
4 tbsp. (50 ml) apple juice, unfiltered
4 tbsp. olive oil
½ tsp. salad herbs
1 pinch black pepper
1 tsp. salt

PREPARATION:

Wash and shred young cabbage into fine thin strips. Wash the lettuce and drain well. Wash, peel and cut the avocado into cubes. Wash the carrot, peel and grate coarsely. For the dressing, combine the lemon juice, apple juice, olive oil, salad herbs, pepper, and salt. Stir with a whisk.

Place the cabbage, lamb's lettuce, grated carrot, sunflower seeds and avocado mix in a salad bowl and pour the dressing and gently stir.

POTATO COCONUT RAITA
2 people

INGREDIENTS:

½ kg waxy potatoes
3 tbsp. shredded coconut
2 tbsp. virgin sesame oil
1 tsp. black mustard seeds
1 cup (250 ml) yogurt (3.6% fat)
⅓ tsp. asafetida
⅓ tsp. sweet paprika powder
1 tbsp. fresh chopped parsley or ander
1 tsp. black salt (kala namak)

PREPARATION:

Boil the potatoes with the skin on until soft and let cool. Meanwhile, combine the yogurt with grated coconut, salt and parsley in a large bowl and stir. Peel the potatoes, dice and add to yogurt sauce. Heat sesame oil in a pan, add mustard seeds and cover the pan. Wait for the mustard seeds to jump; that's the sign that they are ready. Remove the pan from the flame and roast the pepper and asafetida briefly. Pour it all into the yogurt potato raita. Mix well and refrigerate.

ENDIVE POTATO PUMPKIN SEED SALAD
3-4 people

INGREDIENTS:

2 potatoes, boiled in their skins, peeled and thinly sliced
¼ endive salad
2 tbsp. pumpkin seeds, roasted
2 tbsp. virgin pumpkin seed oil
½ lemon, squeezed
½ tsp. salad herbs
1 pinch black pepper
½ tsp. salt
1 pinch of raw sugar

PREPARATION:

Wash, drain and cut the endive into 5 mm thin strips. Place in a large salad bowl. Add all the remaining ingredients and gently stir together.

EGGPLANT (AUBERGINE) AND WALNUT RAITA
4 people

INGREDIENTS:

1 eggplant (aubergine)
2 tbsp. olive oil
50 g walnuts
1 cup (250 ml) plain yogurt
1 tsp. curry powder
½ tsp. sweet paprika powder
1 chili, seeded and finely chopped
⅔ tsp. salt
1 tbsp. parsley, finely chopped

PREPARATION:

Wash the eggplant and cut into large pieces. Heat the oven to 220° C (428° F). Place the eggplant in a baking pan and sprinkle with olive oil. Bake for 15-20 minutes or til tender. Remove and let cool. Chop the walnuts coarsely.

Combine the yogurt with spices, salt and herbs in a bowl, then add the cooled eggplant pieces and walnuts add and mix well. Refrigerate.

MINT RAITA
2 people

INGREDIENTS:

1 cup (250 ml) plain yogurt
10-15 fresh mint leaves or ½ tsp. dried mint
½ tsp. of salt
¼ tsp. black pepper
1 tbsp. olive oil
1 tbsp. sour cream

PREPARATION:

Finely chop the fresh mint leaves and mix immediately with all other ingredients. Refrigerate.

TASTY AND DELICATE BANANA RAITA WITH CILANTRO
4-6 people

INGREDIENTS:

2 bananas, cut into about 5 mm thick slices
1 cup (250) ml plain yogurt
½ tsp. black mustard seeds
2 tbsp. fresh cilantro, coarsely chopped
1 red chili, seeded and chopped
½ tsp. of salt
1 tbsp. sesame oil

PREPARATION:

Heat sesame oil in a small pan and add the mustard seeds. Cover the pan and wait until the mustard seeds no longer jump. When the mustard seeds are gray, they are done, add chili and fry for few seconds.

Mix all ingredients carefully, in a bowl. Finished!

YELLOW LENTIL RAITA
4 people

INGREDIENTS:

1 cup (100 g) chana dal (peeled and split chickpeas), soaked overnight or at least 2 hours - any other type of lentil would be good
1 cup (250) ml plain yogurt
1 tsp. cumin seeds
½ tsp. black mustard seeds
1 tbsp. fresh ginger, finely grated
1 chili, finely chopped
½ tsp. turmeric
⅓ tsp. asafetida
½ tsp. garam masala
1 tbsp. parsley, finely chopped
2 tbsp. sesame oil
1 tsp. salt

PREPARATION:

Wash the chana dal and cook 30-40 minutes in 700 ml of water. The chana dal should be cooked until tender but not falling apart. Rinse with cold water and drain well. In a small pan, heat sesame oil and pour in the mustard seeds. Cover the pan with a lid and wait until the mustard seeds no longer jump. Add the cumin seeds and fry until they turn brown. Add the ginger, turmeric, chili and asafetida and fry briefly. Take the pan off the heat.

Mix the dal, yogurt, parsley, salt and roasted masala in a bowl and sprinkle with garam masala.

CUCUMBER AND CARROT RAITA
4 people

INGREDIENTS:

1 cup (250 ml) plain yogurt
½ of large cucumber, peeled and thinly sliced
1-2 carrots, peeled and finely grated
1 tsp. yellow mustard seeds, coarsely crushed
⅓ tsp. asafetida
1 tsp. curry powder
½ tsp. salt
1 chili, finely chopped
2 tbsp. virgin sesame oil

PREPARATION:

Mix the yogurt with carrots, cucumber, salt and curry powder in a bowl. Heat the sesame oil in a small pan and fry yellow mustard seeds until golden brown. Add the asafetida and chili and fry briefly. Add the masala to the yogurt-cucumber mixture. Add fresh herbs to taste and mix well.

Store in the refrigerator.

Desserts

11.

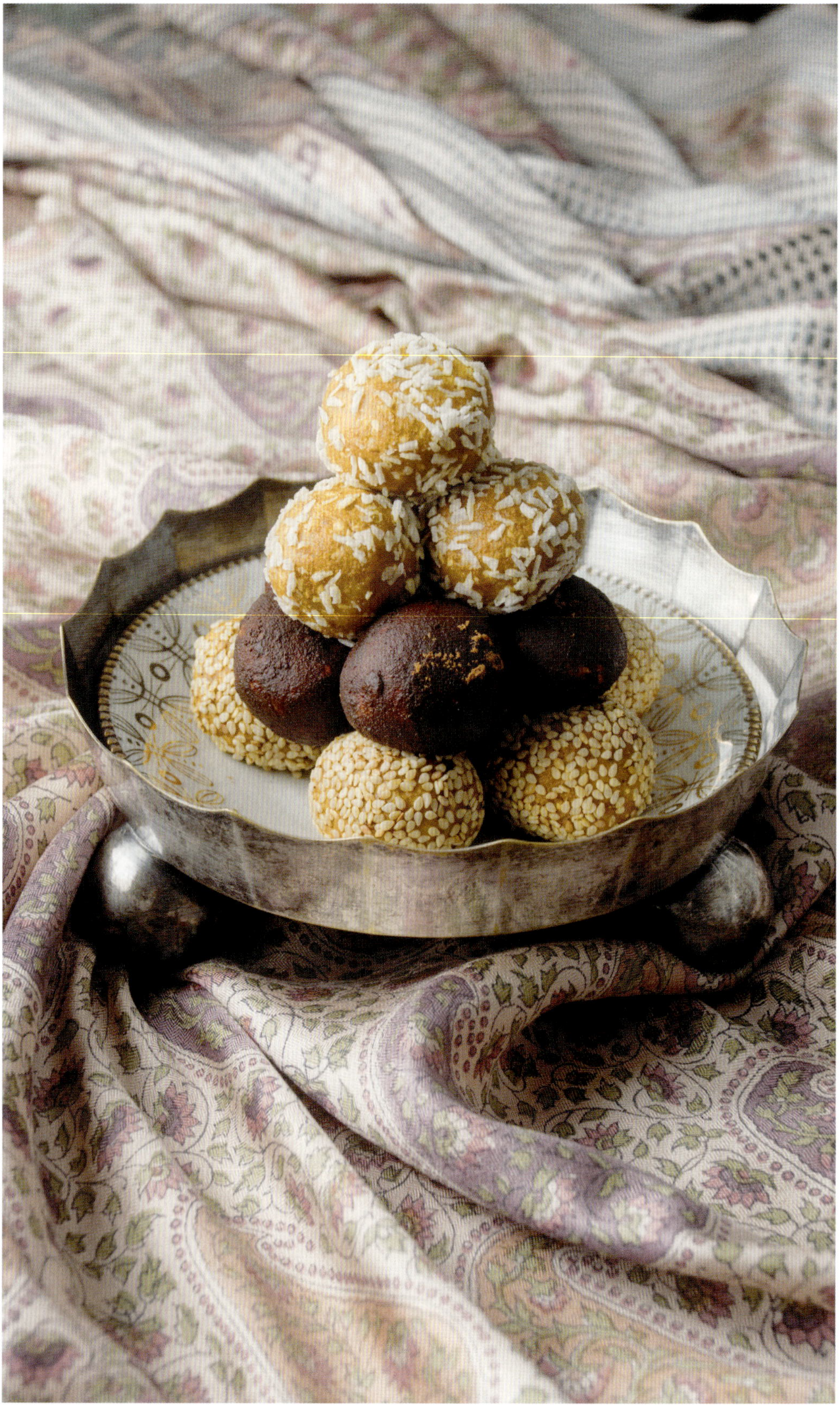

DESSERTS
A little sweetness that you can enjoy with a good conscience

Ayurvedic baking without eggs
Sweets are something very special for Ayurveda. They are gifts of love. With candy, you can appease the cravings and indulge yourself or your loved ones. In India, the sweets are often used as an offering to glorify the divine. Afterwards, these holy sweets (prasadam) are distributed to the devotees.

The desserts in this cookbook are made exclusively with raw cane sugar because white sugar can cause severe physical discomfort and imbalance. Raw cane sugar contains the original minerals and in vitamins and in small amount does not affect our acid-alkaline balance. Taken in small quantities, it works like a "Rasayana", a rejuvenator. Sweet things are especially good for Vata and Pitta types. Kapha people should eat fewer sweets and desserts.

According to Ayurveda, eggs are high in cholesterol and are easily contaminated by bacteria. They do not combine well with carbohydrates. They rot faster than meat in the gastrointestinal tract and disrupt the intestinal flora. You do not need eggs to make cakes, pies, pancakes, dumplings, or strudel. See for yourself how juicy and fluffy the Ayurvedic cakes are. In combination with raw cane sugar, fruits and nuts, they taste great, are cholesterol-free and a delight for everyone.

If you avoid sugar, dates are the best supplement.

BROWNIES (SUGAR-FREE)

INGREDIENTS:

1,5 cups unbleached white cake flour
½ cup cornstarch
1 cup date sugar
2 tbsp. cocoa
⅓ cup melted virgin coconut oil
1 cup coconut milk (or almond milk)
½ lemon, squeezed (or 1 orange)
½ tsp. cardamom powder
½ tsp. ginger powder
⅓ tsp. turmeric
1 tbsp. chickpea flour (serves as emulsifying agent)
1 tsp. pure vanilla extract
½ cup chopped walnuts
1 pinch of salt
2 tsp. of baking powder

PREPARATION:

Mix together date sugar, coconut milk, lemon juice, salt, vanilla, coconut oil, cardamom, ginger, cocoa, turmeric and chickpea flour. Then add the flour, starch, walnuts and baking powder and mix quickly until no more lumps can be seen. Lightly coat the baking pan with coconut oil and sprinkle with flour. Pour the mixture gently into the pan and spread it evenly. Bake 10 minutes at 220° C (428° F). Then turn the oven down to 180-190° C (356° F) and bake for another 25-30 minutes.

ENERGY BALLS

INGREDIENTS:

180 g butter or virgin coconut oil
200 g finely-ground walnuts
180 ml strong roasted barley or grain decaffeinated coffee
250 g raw cane sugar
500 g oatmeal – flakes should be coarsely ground
1 tbsp. cinnamon
1 tsp. pure vanilla extract
200 g coconut flakes

PREPARATION:

Add the butter or coconut fat and the warm coffee substitute to a large bowl. Stir with a whisk until the butter has dissolved. Add in the sugar, cinnamon and nuts and stir.

Add the oatmeal gradually and stir until a solid mass is formed. Chill the mass for a few hours. Form into small balls and roll in coconut flakes. Cover with foil and chill until ready to serve.

SAFFRON HALAVA

INGREDIENTS:

3 cups (¾ l) water
180 g raw cane sugar
15-20 saffron threads, crushed to powder in a mortar and mixed with 3 tbsp. of hot water (so you will get the saffron essence)
1 handful of raisins
180 g butter or 120 g virgin coconut oil
220 g wheat or spelt semolina
2 apples, peeled and sliced
1 handful chopped nuts
1 lemon squeezed

PREPARATION:

Melt the butter in a saucepan over medium heat, add the semolina and roast for 10-15 minutes (constantly stirring) until the meal turns golden brown. Meanwhile, boil the apples and raisins in a saucepan and simmer for about 5 minutes until the apples are cooked through. Add the sugar and nuts. Then add the semolina-butter mixture slowly into the apple-sugar-water and stir carefully. Simmer for another 2 minutes, stirring constantly, until the halava has thickened. Pour the saffron essence and lemon juice in and stir. Let it rest covered for 5 minutes. The halava tastes best when hot. One can also form it into balls and roll them in coconut.

CARAMEL AND SEMOLINA HALAVA
(NOT THE SAME AS THE MIDDLE EASTERN CANDY "HALVAH")

INGREDIENTS:

95 g brown sugar
90 g butter or 70 g virgin coconut oil
110 g wheat or spelt semolina
1-2 tbsp. raisins
1 pinch of salt
2 organic orange peel, grated and squeezed
1.3 cup (350 ml) water

PREPARATION:

Melt the sugar over low heat, pour water and orange juice over it, and cover immediately. Watch out for the steam! Simmer until the sugar has completely dissolved.

Melt the butter and add the semolina and fry for about 10 minutes on low heat. Add the raisins, pinch of salt and orange peel to the sugar mixture, then add the toasted semolina. Simmer 2 minutes until the mixture thickens. Spread the mass on a tray and chill it. You can pour chopped almonds, cocoa powder or grated coconut over it. When it has cooled, cut into pieces and serve. Of course, one can serve halava hot or warm with some fruit or chutneys.

credits to greenmorning

MANGO MASCARPONE CAKE

INGREDIENTS:

Dough:
⅔ cup raw cane sugar
1 cup (250 ml) of organic milk or almond milk,
mixed with the juice of 1 lemon
1 tsp. pure vanilla extract
2 tsp. baking powder
2 carrots, finely grated
1 tsp. cardamom
2 cups organic unrefined white cake flour
⅓ cup (100 ml) sunflower oil, or organic melted butter or coconut fat
zest and juice from 1 orange

Icing:
250 g mascarpone
250 g ricotta
4-5 tbsp. raw cane sugar
5-6 tbsp. mango purée (enough so that the icing stays firm)

PREPARATION:

Mix the sugar, milk, orange zest and juice, vanilla, oil and cardamom together. Add in the flour and baking powder and stir vigorously until there are no more lumps. Then add in the grated carrots. Coat the baking pan well with butter and dust with flour. Put the mixture into the pan carefully and bake 10 minutes at 220° C (428° F). Then lower the heat to 180° C (356° F) and bake for another 25-30 minutes. Let the cake cool.

For the icing: Mix all ingredients well and spread evenly over the cake. Immediately refrigerate.

BESAN LADDU
Sweets made with chickpea flour)

INGREDIENTS:

180-190 g virgin coconut oil
250 g chickpea flour
½ tsp. cardamom powder
1 tbsp. carob powder (optional)
125 g raw cane sugar, finely ground in a coffee grinder
4 tbsp. crushed sesame seeds

PREPARATION:

Melt the coconut fat in a frying pan over low heat, stir in the chickpea flour with a wooden spoon. After about 15 minutes of constant stirring, the flour should be roasted and have a nutty smell. Remove the pan from the heat and add the sugar into it. Allow to cool (about 15 minutes). Now stir in all the other ingredients. Place the doughy mass on a lightly greased sheet and smooth it out. Laddu should rest overnight. Cut into small squares and serve.

DELICIOUS APPLE CAKE WITHOUT DOUGH

INGREDIENTS:

150 g whole-grain spelt flour
150 g semolina
150 g raw cane sugar, finely ground in a coffee grinder
120 g virgin coconut oil
1 tsp. pure vanilla extract
1 tsp. cinnamon powder
zest and juice from 1 lemon
1/3 tsp. of salt
1.5 kg apples
sunflower seeds for sprinkling (optional)

PREPARATION:

Grease a deep baking dish (casserole: 20 x 30 cm). Mix the whole-grain flour, semolina, lemon zest, sugar, salt, vanilla and cinnamon together. Divide the dough into 3 parts and set aside. Wash the apples, peel and grate. Pour lemon juice over the apples and divide into 2 parts. Set the oven, using the upper and lower heating elements and heat to 200° C (392° F). Melt the coconut fat. Distribute the first part of the dry semolina- flour-sugar mixture in the baking pan and cover with the first half of the grated apples. Then spread the second layer of the mixture and cover with the second part of the apples. Now cover with the third layer of the dry dough and decorate and spread half of the coconut fat with a spoon on the cake. Bake for 25 minutes at 180°C (356° F). Take the cake from the oven and baste with the other half of the melted coconut fat, sprinkle sunflower seeds evenly and bake another 25 minutes. Finished!

CARROT ALMONDS HALAVA

INGREDIENTS:

500 g carrots
50 g butter or 1 tbsp. virgin coconut fat
250 ml milk or almond milk
100 g raw cane sugar
2 tbsp. raisins
2 tbsp. almonds, peeled and cut into strips
½ tsp. cardamom, ground

PREPARATION:

Peel the carrots and grate finely or grind in a food processor. In a saucepan, heat the butter and fry the carrots over moderate heat for 5 minutes. Pour in the milk and cook about 25 minutes on a low heat until the halava thickens, stirring occasionally. Add in the sugar, raisins, almonds and cardamom and simmer another 10-15 minutes while stirring constantly so that the mass is very thick and compact. The milk should be completely thickened and the carrots should have a beautiful dark-orange color. The halvah can be served in bowls and enjoyed hot or spread on a baking sheet, cooled and then cut into pieces, or shaped into small dumplings.

COCONUT PANCAKES WITHOUT EGGS

INGREDIENTS:

1 cup (250 ml) coconut milk or almond milk
⅔ cup (170 ml) of water or mineral water (as needed)
1 cup (100 g) whole-grain spelt or wheat flour
1.5 cup (150 g) unrefined cake flour
½ tsp. salt
zest and juice from 1 lemon
½ tsp. turmeric
1 tsp. chickpea flour
sunflower oil

PREPARATION:

Mix all the ingredients with a whisk until smooth. The dough should not be too runny or too thick, so that it easily flows and does not stick. Pour a small amount of oil (1 tsp.) into a pancake pan. Once the oil is hot, pour in some pancake batter and cook until it is golden brown on both sides. For the filling, you can use jams, or sweeten with raw sugar cane or fruit juice concentrate. Fillings of fruit purée, maple syrup, or nut cream are especially good.

APPLE JELLY CAKE WITH WHIPPED CREAM

INGREDIENTS:

Dough:
1 cup whole-grain flour - spelt or wheat
1 cup unrefined cake flour
⅓ cup melted virgin coconut fat
¾ cup raw cane sugar
1 pinch of salt
2 tsp. baking powder
1 cup coconut or almond milk - mixed with 2 tbsp. lemon juice until thick sour milk is produced
1 tbsp. chickpea flour
3 tbsp. cocoa or 1 tbsp. of carob powder
1 tsp. ground cinnamon
⅓ tsp. ground cloves
½ tsp. turmeric

Jelly:
1 kg of apples, peeled and very thinly sliced
⅓ cup (90 ml) organic apple juice, unfiltered
2 heaping tbsp. cornstarch
100 g raw cane sugar
1 tsp. cinnamon
½ lemon, squeezed

Whipped Cream (optional):
1 tsp. vanilla extract
1.2 cup (300 ml) heavy cream
⅓ tsp. cardamom powder

PREPARATION:

In a bowl, mix together the sour milk, melted coconut fat, chickpea flour, a pinch of salt, raw cane sugar, vanilla extract, turmeric, cloves, cinnamon, and cocoa. The sugar should be mixed until it dissolves completely. When adding the cocoa and carob, be careful that no lumps are formed. The best way is to pass them through a sieve.

Add in the flour and baking powder and stir briefly but vigorously. The thick dough should be free of lumps. Grease a cake pan and dust with a little flour or semolina. Pour the cake batter gently and spread evenly with a kitchen spatula. Do not stir the base of casserole as this will cause the cake to burn. Using the top and bottom heating elements, heat up the oven to 220° C (428° F). Bake for 10 minutes. Lower the heat to 180-190° C (356° F) and bake for another 25-30 minutes.

In a saucepan, cover the apples with 3 tbsp. of apple juice and cook 10 minutes, until the apples are soft. In a bowl, mix the rest of apple juice, lemon juice, cinnamon, and cornstarch and then add to the apples. Add in the raw cane sugar, cook for 2 minutes, stirring constantly with a whisk until the mixture forms a thick "custard." Pour the hot apple mixture over the finished cake and spread evenly. Let the cake cool. Beat the whipping cream with vanilla and cardamom powder until stiff and spread over the cooled cake.

Decorate with grated nuts or cinnamon and cocoa.

Refrigerate for 2 hours.

SHRIKAND - THICK YOGURT WITH SAFFRON AND ORANGE ZEST

INGREDIENTS:

4 cups (1 l) of natural yogurt
½ tsp. saffron threads
orange zest
80 g raw cane sugar

PREPARATION:

Place a large sieve in a large bowl. Fold a muslin cloth 3 times and place it in the sieve. The cloth should be large enough so that it can absorb the whole liter of yogurt and you can grab the ends outside of the sieve. Tie the ends of the cloth together and hang it so that the liquid will drip into the bowl. Drain at least 4-8 hours. The yogurt should then be very thick. One-half to one-third of the original quantity should remain in the cloth. Remove the yogurt with a spatula from the cloth and place in a bowl.

   Grind the saffron threads with a stone mortar and pestle and then spoon the saffron into the thick yogurt. Add in the orange zest and cane sugar and stir until fluffy with a whisk.

PLUM LEMON CARDAMOM CAKE

INGREDIENTS:

20 plums, washed, pitted and halved
1 cup whole-grain flour - spelt or wheat
1 cup unrefined cake flour
⅓ cup melted virgin coconut fat
¾ cup raw cane sugar
1 pinch of salt
2 tsp. baking powder
1 cup coconut milk and 2 tbsp. lemon juice mixed together
1 tbsp. chickpea flour
grated zest of 1 organic lemon
½ tsp. turmeric
½ tsp. cardamom
1 tsp. pure vanilla extract
3 tbsp. blackberry or red currant jam

PREPARATION:

In a bowl, add the coconut milk mixed with lemon juice, melted coconut fat, chickpea flour, a pinch of salt, raw cane sugar, vanilla, turmeric, lemon zest and cardamom. Stir until the sugar is completely dissolved. Using the top and bottom heating elements, set the oven to 220° C (428° F). Add in the flour and baking powder and stir with short, strong strokes. The thick mass should be free of lumps. Prepare a cake pan with grease and dust with a little flour or semolina. Gently pour the cake batter into the pan and spread evenly with a kitchen spatula. Do not touch the pie crust, otherwise the cake will burn on this part. Place the halved plums carefully on top. Slide into the hot oven and bake at 200° C (392° F) for 10 minutes. Lower the heat to 180-190° C (356° F) and bake for another 25-30 minutes. Boil the blackberry or red currant jam with 4 tbsp. water in a small saucepan, stir and pour over the hot cake. Let it rest for at least 2 hours. The cake will shine beautifully and the plums will still look fresh on the next day.

CHOCOLATE NUT CHERRY JAM BALLS

INGREDIENTS:

2 cups whole-grain flour - spelt or wheat
⅓ cup sunflower oil
¾ cup raw cane sugar
1 pinch of salt
2 tsp. baking powder
1 cup coconut milk and 2 tbsp. lemon juice, combine

1 tbsp. chickpea flour
4 tbsp. cocoa or 2 tbsp. carob powder
1 tsp. pure vanilla extract
½ tsp. turmeric
4 tbsp. cherry jam
a little rum extract

PREPARATION:

In a bowl, mix together the coconut milk combined with lemon juice, oil, chickpea flour, a pinch of salt, cane sugar, vanilla, turmeric, cloves, cinnamon and cocoa. Mix well so that the sugar is completely dissolved. Take care that the carob or cocoa does not form lumps. It is best to pass the mixture through a sieve. Stir in the flour and baking powder with short, strong strokes.

The thick mass should be free of lumps. Grease a cake pan and dust with a little flour or semolina. Gently pour the cake batter into the pan and spread evenly with a spatula. Do not disturb the bottom of the cake, otherwise the cake will burn.

Slide the cake into the hot oven and bake 10 minutes at 200°C (392° F), using the top and bottom heating elements. Lower the heat to 180-190° C (356° F) and bake for another 25-30 minutes. Let the cake cool for 20 minutes, then it remove from the pan and place in a plastic bowl. Crumble the cake with the fingers, add in the cherry jam and rum flavouring and mix well. Gently form small balls and roll the balls in grated walnuts.

The balls will keep for 3 days in the refrigerator.

APPLE RICOTTA PIE

INGREDIENTS:

Dough:
250 g butter or 180 g virgin coconut oil
270 g whole-grain flour
1-2 tbsp. of coconut milk or almond milk
½ tsp. of salt

Apple Filling:
1 ½ kg peeled and grated apples
4-5 tbsp. sugar
1 tbsp. cinnamon powder

Ricotta Filling:
250 g ricotta or fresh farmer cheese
1 tbsp. cornstarch
⅓ cup (80 ml) heavy cream
1 tsp. pure vanilla extract
½ tsp. turmeric
zest from 1 lemon, grated
3 tbsp. raw cane sugar

PREPARATION:

Mix all the dough ingredients and knead well until a dough is formed. Spread half of the dough in a baking pan and bake at 180°C (356° F) for 10 minutes. Take the baking pan out of the oven and place the apple filling on top (mixed grated apples with sugar and cinnamon powder). For the cheese filling, mix all ingredients until they are free of lumps and spread it on top of the apple filling evenly with a tablespoon. Sprinkle the second half of the cookie dough on top and bake at 180° C (356° F) for an additional 40 minutes.

ALMOND RICE CARDAMOM PUDDING

INGREDIENTS:

50 grams of almonds, peeled and crushed to fine powder
3 tbsp. basmati rice, finely ground (best to use a coffee grinder)
3 tbsp. raw cane sugar
1 ¾ cup (400 ml) milk or 1 cup (250 ml) and ⅔ cup (150 ml) coconut milk and 150 ml water)
½ tsp. cardamom powder
⅓ cup (100 ml) mango pulp or any other fruit pulp

PREPARATION:

Pour all ingredients in one saucepan and simmer while stirring occasionally for about 5-10 minutes until it has thickened.

Pour into dessert bowls, let it cool down and garnish with fruit pulp.

TAPIOCA CARDAMOM PUDDING WITH COCONUT MILK

INGREDIENTS:

3 tbsps Tapioca or Sago
2 tbsps raw cane sugar
1 ¼ cup (300 ml) coconut milk and
⅓ cup (100 ml water)
½ tsp cardamom powder
⅓ cup (100 ml) mangopulp or any other fruitpulp

PREPARATION:

Pour coconut milk, water and cardamom in one saucepan to cook. Add tapioca. While stirring continuously, simmer for 5-10 minutes and let thicken slightly. Continue to stir until the tapioca becomes tender and translucent, 2-3 minutes. If the porridge becomes too thick for your liking, you can thin it out with more water or coconut milk.

Pour into dessert bowls, let it cool down and garnish with fruitpulp or fresh mango.

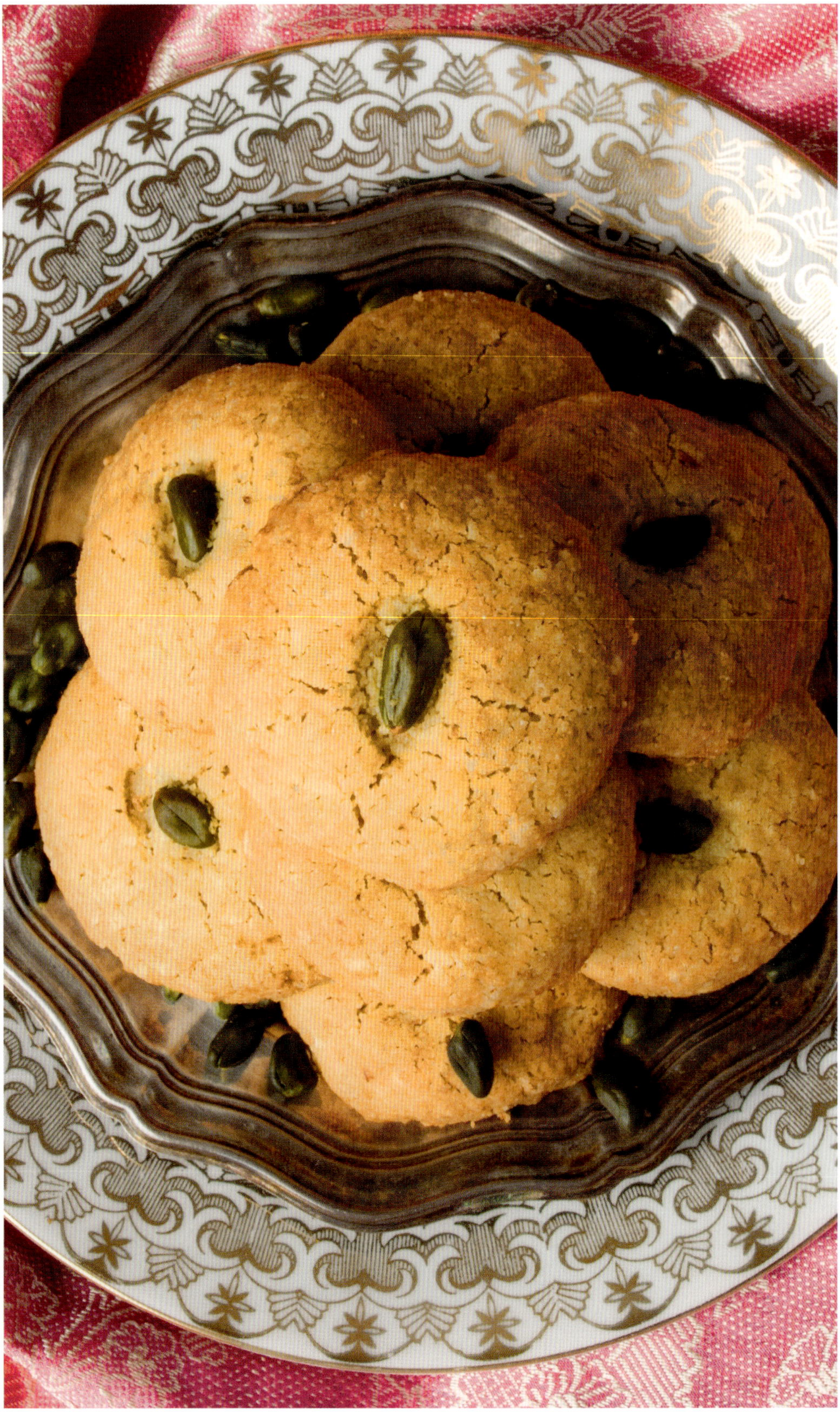

NANKHATAI (AYURVEDIC COOKIES)
(makes around 15-20 medium sized cookies)

INGREDIENTS:

260 g (1 ½ cup) whole spelt or wheat flour
25 g (1,5 big tbsp) chickpeaflour
25 g (1 big tbsp) semolina
200 g virgin coconut fat
110 g (½ cup) raw cane sugar (grounded to powder in a electric coffee grinder
1 pinch of salt
⅓ tsp. baking powder
1 tbsp. grated coconut
½ tsp. cardamom powder
1 pinch of saffron
80 g grounded walnuts
20 pistachio to decorate

PREPARATION:

Mix spelt flour, chickpea flour, semolina, cardamom, saffron, baking powder, salt and fat together. Now add coconut and walnuts and try to form a dough. If needed, add some coconut milk (just 1-2 tbsp.) to make nice dough. Preheat the oven to 180° C (356° F). Grease a baking tray with coconut fat and dust it with a tiny bit of flour. Make tiny balls. Slightly flatten the balls on the baking tray and put one pistachio in each.
Bake for 12-15 minutes. Nankhatai should be golden brown when they are ready. Let them cool for 10 minutes at least, before taking them out of the baking tray.

BANANABREAD SUGAR-FREE

INGREDIENTS:

700 g peeled and mashed Bananas
80 g (⅔ cup) oat flakes
150 g (1 cup) whole wheat or spelt flour
100 g (½ cup) raisins
½ tsp. cinnamon
½ tsp. ginger powder
¼ tsp. clove powder
½ cup almonds (without skin, grounded)
½ tsp. pure almond extract (optional)
1 pinch of salt
⅓ tsp. baking powder
½ cup melted virgin coconut fat

PREPARATION:

Preheat the oven to 180° C (356° F), grease a baking tray with coconut fat and dust it with a tiny bit of flour. Mix all ingredients together in a smooth dough. Bake for 40 to 50 minutes, or until a toothpick inserted into the center comes out clean. Let the bread cool in the loaf pan for 10 minutes, then transfer it to a wire rack to cool for 20 minutes before slicing.

Drinks

12.

DRINKS
Warm in the winter and refreshing in the summer.

According to Ayurveda, it is best to sip a small cup of warm water, herbal tea or highly diluted lassi during the meal. Ice-cold drinks or milk should be avoided when eating because they dilute the gastric juices and therefore stop the digestion.

A chai or yogi tea, made in the traditional way with milk and a piece of cake in the afternoon makes a wonderful snack. Almond milk is an excellent breakfast drink. Ginger and orange tea is ideal for in between, and hot spiced milk can calm us down before bedtime.

REFRESHING GINGER-APPLE DRINK

INGREDIENTS:

a 5-10 cm piece of ginger, finely grated and juice squeezed out of it
2 cups (500 ml) apple juice, unfiltered
½ lime, squeezed

PREPARATION:

In a jug or pitcher, combine the apple juice, lime juice and ginger juice. Mix together and chill.

FRUITY COCONUT MILK

INGREDIENTS:

2 cups (500 ml) coconut milk
4 cups (1 l) pineapple juice
1 tbsp. maple syrup

PREPARATION:

Mix all ingredients with a mixer and whisk until frothy.

LIME ROSE DRINK

INGREDIENTS:
2 lime, squeezed
1 shot rosewater (1-2 tbsp.)
1 tbsp. raw cane sugar or maple syrup
3 cups (¾ l) water
1 tbsp. grenadine syrup or some fresh grenadine juice

PREPARATION:

Place all the ingredients in a bowl and whisk well.

SAFFRON LEMONADE

MANGO-LASSI

VEDA-COLA

GINGER-APPLE DRINK

SAFFRON LEMONADE

INGREDIENTS:

15 saffron threads
2 lemons, squeezed
2 tbsp. raw cane sugar
4 cups (1 l) of water

PREPARATION:

Crush the saffron threads in a stone mortar and pestle. Using a spoon, transfer the saffron into a glass jug. Add all the other ingredients and give it a good whisking. You can use 2-3 tbsp. of hot water to remove all of the saffron from the mortar.

VEDA PUNCH

INGREDIENTS:

4 cups (1 l) of red grape juice, unfiltered
a little rum extract
1 tbsp. fresh ginger, finely grated
4 cloves, whole
5 green cardamom pods, coarsely crushed
1 cinnamon stick, coarsely crushed
1 cup (250 ml) of water

PREPARATION:

Boil 250 ml of water. Add the ginger, cloves, cardamom and cinnamon and simmer for about 10 minutes. Add the red grape juice and rum extract. Strain the mixture and serve hot. Finished!

HOMEMADE YOGI TEA - CHAI

INGREDIENTS:

3 cups (740 ml) of water
2 cinnamon sticks, coarsely crushed
5-10 cardamom pods, coarsely crushed
4-6 cloves
1 tbsp. grated ginger
1 tbsp. Rooibos tea
200 ml milk
a little raw cane sugar or maple syrup

PREPARATION:

Mix all ingredients except milk, sugar, and Rooibos tea. Let it simmer for 20 minutes until the liquid has reduced by one-third or by half. Add the Rooibos tea, milk, and sugar, bring to a boil again and strain.
 Finished!

HOT EVENING MILK WITH PISTACHIOS AND RAISINS

INGREDIENTS:

200 ml milk (or almond milk)
1 tsp. raw pistachios, unsalted
1 tbsp. raisins, unsulfured
1 pinch of nutmeg
a few drops of ghee and turmeric (optional)

PREPARATION:

Boil the raisins in 50 ml of water and simmer for 2 minutes. Put aside. Boil milk until creamy. Add all the ingredients together and mix until creamy with a mixer.
Serve immediately.

GINGER ORANGE TEA

INGREDIENTS:

a 10 cm piece of ginger, grated
2 oranges, squeezed
½ lemon, squeezed
3 cups of water
2 tbsp. maple syrup

PREPARATION:

Bring the water to a boil and pour in the grated ginger. Let it simmer for about 3 minutes. Strain the ginger tea and add the orange juice, lemon juice and maple syrup.

VEDA-COLA WITH TAMARIND

INGREDIENTS:

2 tbsp. tamarind paste
⅓ tsp. licorice powder
80 g raw cane sugar
4 cups (1 l) soda water

PREPARATION:

Put all ingredients in a jug and whisk well.

MANGO LASSI

INGREDIENTS:

1 cup (250 ml) plain organic yogurt
1 cup (250 ml) water
⅓ cup (100 ml) mango pulp
or a mango, puréed
1 tbsp. raw cane sugar or honey
1 shot of rosewater
½ tsp. cardamom powder

PREPARATION:

Blend all the ingredients with a whisk or blender, until the surface of lassi is frothy. Finished!

SALTY LASSI WITH MINT

INGREDIENTS:

10 fresh mint leaves or
½ tsp. dried mint, crushed
1 cup (250 ml) plain organic yogurt
1 cup (250 ml) water or soda water
½ tsp. salt

PREPARATION:

Wash the mint and chop/grind finely. Add all the other ingredients in a blender and mix until frothy.

SALTY LASSI DRINK WITH CUMIN

INGREDIENTS:

1 cup (250 ml) plain organic yogurt or buttermilk
1 cup (250 ml) water
1 tsp. cumin seeds
1 lemon, squeezed
½ tsp. salt
1 pinch black pepper
1 pinch of raw cane sugar

PREPARATION:

Dry roast the cumin in a pan (without oil), until the cumin turns a dark brown color and emits a very fragrant smell. Grind the roasted cumin finely in a coffee grinder or a stone mortar. Mix all ingredients with a mixer or blender until the beverage is frothy.

LEMON HONEY DRINK

INGREDIENTS:

½ lemon, squeezed
1 cup (250 ml) warm, but not hot water
1 tsp. honey
1 tsp. crushed flaxseed

PREPARATION:

Mix everything together and drink immediately.

This drink strengthens the digestive and liver activity and is best enjoyed early in the morning.

ALMOND MILK

INGREDIENTS:

1 cup (100 g) almonds, peeled
⅓ tsp. cardamom, crushed
2 cups (500 ml) hot water or as needed to get milky structure
1 tbsp. honey
1 dash of rosewater (optional)

PREPARATION:

Pour the hot water over the almonds. Allow to cool. Add all the other ingredients and blend until creamy. Strain it if you like or drink it as is.

Healthy gut – happy life

12.

INTESTINAL HEALTH

Traditional medicine as Ayurveda has strong historical and cultural roots. The climate in India is warm, so there is no need to preserve foods for the cold season. In Europe we need to heat to survive long winters. Fermented or cultured foods are heating and can aggravate pitta. This effect however only happens when fermented foods are taken in excess. Even in the summer in small amounts as „condiments", fermented foods can boost digestive strength.

The intestinal system is the engine of our life. Not only does it provide fuel through digestion, it also affects many processes from head to toe. If the bowel is out of balance, it affects the entire body. Our lifestyle decisively governs whether the gut is fine or not. In our modern age with the oversupply of industrially-manufactured foods and a variety of harmful environmental influences, it is not easy to keep the intestines healthy. But there are effective measures for improving and maintaining gut health.

Abstaining from gluten, sugar and milk for a few weeks or months can greatly support the renewal of the intestinal flora.

Natural fermentation as the basis for a good intestinal flora microbiome

Probiotic lactic acid bacteria such as lactobacilli and Bifidobacterium are living microorganisms that bring a health benefit to humans when they are consumed in sufficient quantities. It is already known that an out-of-balance intestinal flora plays a role in the development of diseases. In addition to a healthy, balanced diet, sufficient exercise and stress avoidance, the use of medically-approved probiotics is recommended to restore the balance in the intestine. Through the supply of viable, probiotic intestinal bacteria, the "good" gut bacteria receive reinforcement. Probiotic vegetables, such as sauerkraut, should be eaten raw in small amounts and not boiled. Pasteurized sauerkraut preparations from the supermarket are "dead", and so no longer contain live lactic acid bacteria. The home-made sauerkraut pays for itself.

SAUERKRAUT

INGREDIENTS:
- 1 kg cabbage
- 1-2 carrots
- 2% salt (per kg of vegetables = 20 g of salt)
- 4 bay leaves
- 2-3 cloves
- 10 juniper berries
- 1 tsp of mix-spices: caraway seeds, anise, fennel, peppercorns

PREPARATION:

Wash the cabbage and carrots, but put aside the 2 outer cabbage leaves. Cut into thin strips in the food processor or with a slicer. Put in a large bowl. Grate carrots, add to the cabbage and mix well with your hands. Add salt and mix until the juices come out.

Add all spices.

Pack the mixture into a large jar, mash it down well, so that no air is trapped and everything is under the sauerkraut juice.
Cover everything with the 2 large cabbage leaves and close the lid well. Label (ingredients and date). Leave to ferment for 4 days in a warm place, then place in the cellar. After 3-5 weeks the sauerkraut is ready. It becomes more and more aromatic due to longer maturation. You take a small amount (2-3 spoonfuls) a day, regularly.

RED BEET "KWASS"

is a traditional fermented beverage from Ukraine. Kvass is an excellent tonic for the blood, supports the digestion, makes the body more alkaline, cleanses the liver and is used in treating kidney stones.

INGREDIENTS:

2 medium-sized beets
1 liter of pure water
1 tbsp salt
2 capsules of probiotics powder
1 turmeric root and 1 small piece of ginger (finely sliced)
½ tsp black pepper (roughly crushed)

PREPARATION:

Thoroughly wash and brush the beets (if possible, do not peel). Cut into medium-sized pieces. Put this in a large Mason jar. Mix water, salt and probiotics powder and pour over the beets and spices. Close the top. Allow the beets to ferment for 1 week in a warm place, then place in the refrigerator and enjoy a shot glass (20-40 ml) of it on an empty stomach every day (let it stand for about half an hour before drinking).

GLUTEN-FREE RECIPES FOR BREAD AND CAKE

BUCKWHEAT RICE BREAD
(natural fermentation with sourdough)

Buckwheat is pseudo-cereal because it does not belong to edible grains like real cereals. It is related to sorrel, knotweed, and rhubarb. Buckwheat is grown in Europe, but it has disappeared from everyday life. It is called an "alternative grain". Buckwheat is delicious when briefly dry-roasted in the oven at 180° C for 15-20 minutes. This gives it gets a wonderful nutty and full-bodied taste. It can be cooked like rice (with much less water: 1 cup of buckwheat - 1.5 cups of water) and can be served with stir-fries, curries and stews as a side dish. Buckwheat is also good for soups, pancakes (blinis) or added to nuggets.

INGREDIENTS:

2 cups of buckwheat and 1 cup of rice
1 cup of mixed seeds (hemp seeds, pumpkin seeds, sunflower seeds), dry-roasted
1-2 teaspoons salt
1 tsp of mix-spices: anise, fennel, cumin and coriander
3 tablespoons coconut fat (melted)

PREPARATION:

Soak the buckwheat and rice in water for 2 hours, rinse well and grind in a mixer with a little water to a thick paste. Put the paste overnight in a bowl, covered with a dishcloth. The next day, mix the fermented buckwheat rice dough with other ingredients and bake in a bread mold (greased and dusted with flour, or with baking paper) for about 45 minute at 180° C.

CAROB-BUCKWHEAT CAKE

INGREDIENTS:

1 cup of buckwheat flour (if possible self-ground from whole buckwheat)
1 cup of almond or walnut flour (self-ground)
1 crushed banana
1 tbsp carob powder
1/3 cup of melted coconut fat
½ cup of date syrup or maple syrup
1 pinch of salt
2 tsp baking powder
1 cup of coconut milk or almond milk
1 organic lemon – juice and zest
1 tablespoon chickpea flour
1/2 tsp turmeric
1 pinch of black pepper
1/2 tsp cardamom
pinch of vanilla

PREPARATION:

ICING: 80 g of cocoa butter or coconut oil, 40 g of carob powder, 3 tablespoons of maple syrup, 60-80 ml of boiling water

In a bowl, stir in the vegetable milk, melted coconut oil, crushed banana, chickpea flour, a pinch of salt, date syrup, vanilla, turmeric, lemon zest, lemon juice, carob powder, pepper and cardamom. Preheat the oven (top and bottom heat) to 200 °C. Add the flour and baking powder separately. While doing so, stir the mixture briskly until it totally blended and lump-free. Spread a cake pan with grease and sprinkle with a bit of flour or semolina.

Carefully pour in the mixture and spread evenly with a kitchen spatula. Do not touch the cake bottom, otherwise the cake will burn. Bake for 35 minutes at 180°C.

For the icing: combine all the ingredients together, bring to a boil and pour over the cake evenly. You can use a hand blender to avoid lumps and to emulsify fat and hot water.

APPLE-CARROT-ALMOND CAKE

INGREDIENTS:

250 g carrots finely grated
150 g of apple grated
Add 1 tbsp lemon juice
Add 50 g raisins or dried fruits as you like
200 g of ground almonds
125 g rice flour (made from basmati rice, ground)
3 teaspoons baking powder
1 pinch of salt
½ teaspoon cinnamon
¼ teaspoon cardamom
Knife tip of clove powder
80 g of maple syrup
125 ml almond milk or fresh orange juice
100 ml of almond oil

PREPARATION:

In a bowl, mix all the dry ingredients (rice flour, almonds, spices and baking powder). Mix lemon juice, almond oil, maple syrup and almond milk until homogeneous and then gently add in the flour. Fold in the carrot and apple mixture. Use a cake pan with 22 cm diameter. Bake for 35-40 minutes at 180°C in the middle of the oven, using both the top/bottom heat.

Check-List

RECOMMENDATIONS FOR YOUR HOME PANTRY BEFORE YOU START WITH AYURVEDIC COOKING

SPICES	LEGUMES / LENTILS
Turmeric (powder)	Beluga lentils
Coriander seeds	Chickpeas and chickpea flour
Black cumin seeds	Dupuy lentils
Cumin seeds	Mountain lentils
Asafoetida (powder)	Brown lentils
Fenugreek (seeds and powder)	Yellow lentils
Fennel seeds (green)	Red lentils
Ajwain (wild celery seeds)	Green lentils
Anise seeds	**Mung Dal** (yellow)
Cinnamon (sticks and powder)	**Mung beans** (green)
Cloves (whole)	Urad Dal
Cardamom (whole, green) **and powder**	Runner beans
Nutmeg (whole)	Pinto beans
Ginger (fresh root)	Kidney beans
Star anise, mace and fennel (all in powder form)	

GRAINS	OILS
Spelt flour (pastry for cake or whole-grain for bread)	**FOR COOKING AT HIGH HEAT:**
Also good for bread and cakes: Emmer, Einkorn, Kamut	**Organic ghee** (clarified butter)
Barley (whole grain)	**Coconut oil** (native)
Millet (whole grain)	**Sesame oil** (native, light)
Buckwheat (whole grain)	**Sunflower oil** (the one with high heat stability, suitable for frying)
Corn grits	**FOR REFINING, VEGETABLE STEWS AND SALADS:**
Oatmeal	Olive oil
Basmati rice	Linseed oil
Whole grain brown rice	Pumpkin seed oil
Grünkern	Argan oil
	Sesame oil (dark, roasted) for wok cooking (add at the end)
	Walnut oil and almond oil

SWEETENERS	SALT	NUTS AND SEEDS
Raw cane sugar	Himalayan rock salt	Walnuts, Almonds
Dates	Kala Namak (black salt)	Hazelnuts (roasted)
Date syrup		Cashews
Date sugar (dry)		Pine nuts
Maple syrup		Pistachios
Honey (do not heat)		Sesame seeds
		Flax seeds (linseed)
		Sunflower seeds
		Pumpkin seeds
		Tahini sesame paste
		Almond butter

ABOUT THE AUTHOR

Sandra Hartmann, holistic Ayurveda nutritionist, chef and book author, born in 1973 in Croatia, has 30 years of experience in Ayurvedic cuisine. In the 1990s, she spent 7 years in Vedic monasteries across Europe and India learning bhakti yoga meditation and Ayurvedic cooking. The alchemy of cooking and the healing power of Ayurveda fascinated the talented cook and she dutifully studied under the guidance of Vedic Brahmins (priests). The meditative aspect and special awareness required for cooking as well as the role of water as the main element that absorbs and transports the cook's energies into foods, have greatly influenced Sandra.

Because only Brahmins are allowed to cook in Hindu monasteries, Sandra underwent rigorous training and education to obtain Brahmanic initiation and was thus authorised to cook in temple kitchens. For seven years Sandra honed her skills as an Ayurvedic chef by cooking for thousands of bhakti yoga students and their teachers. She then went on to specialise as a chef for Ayurvedic Panchakarma treatments, pure vegetarian restaurants and catering for special events. In 2007, Sandra qualified as a consultant in dietetics and health by the European Academy of Ayurveda.

Sandra is the founder of the first Ayurvedic Cooking School of Vienna where she dedicates her life to share her knowledge and experience by running workshops and training future Ayurvedic chefs.

In 2009, Sandra published her first Ayurveda cookbook which has become bestseller in German: "Der Schatz der Ayurveda Küche" (The Treasure of the Ayurveda Cuisine). The Ayurveda Alchemist Cookbook is new, updated version written with love and dedication to increase consciousness of people trough hidden power of sacred food. With its abundant source of information on spices and herbs, it is a great reference book on authentic Ayurvedic cooking and nutrition. The quality of the food you eat creates your state of mind, emotions and consciousness.

Let this book serve you in your endeavor to create food that will improve your wellbeing.

For more Details: **www.ayurveda-alchemist.com**
Contact: **info@ayurveda-alchemist.at**

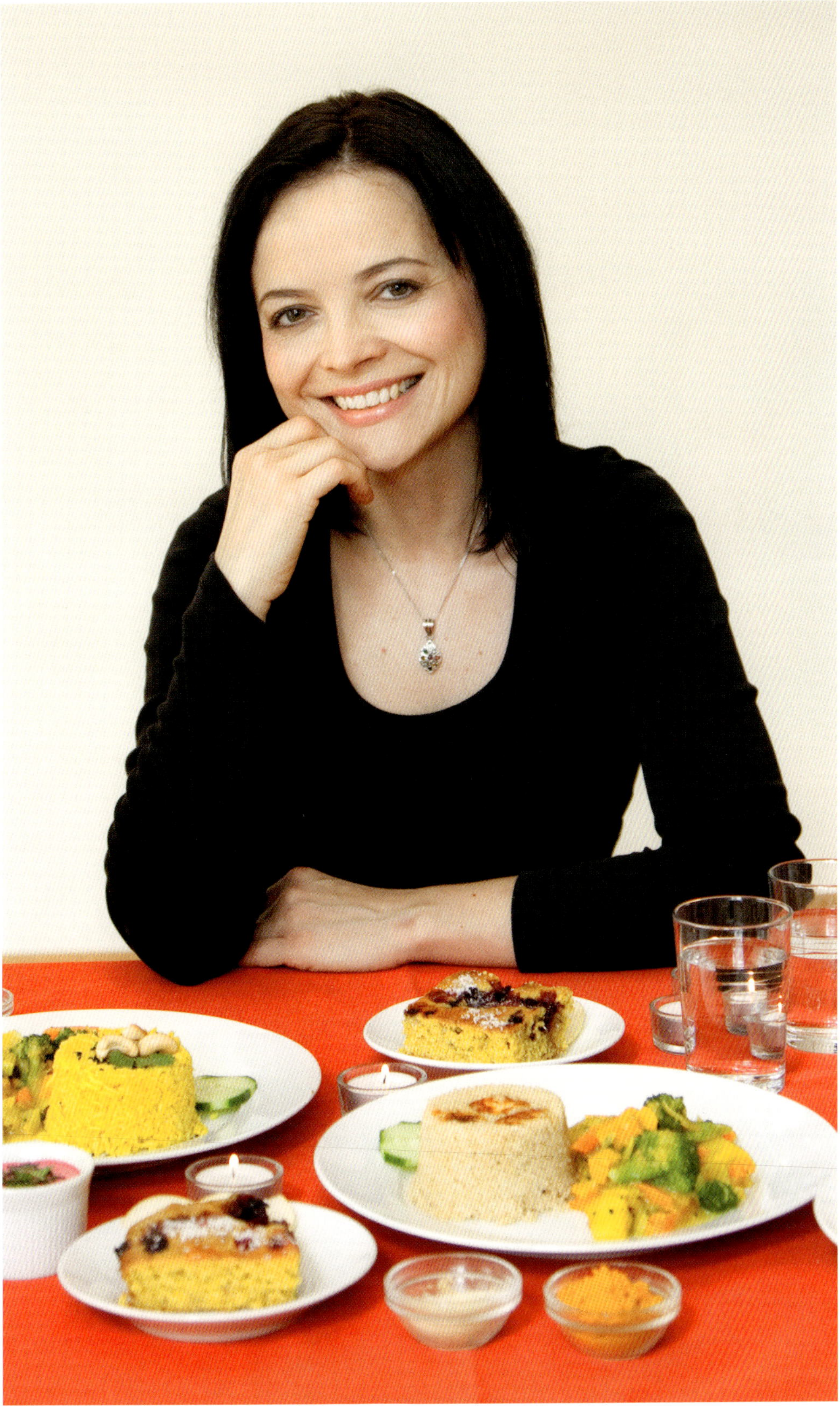

LITERATURE:

Dr. Bharat Aggarwal & Debora Yost: "Healing Spices"
David Frawley: "Ayurvedic Healing - A Comprehensive Guide"
Vasant Lad: "Ayurveda: The Science of Self Healing"
Swami A.C. Bhaktivedanta Prabhupada: "Bhagavad Gita as it is"
David Dr. Frawley: "Ayurveda and the Mind: The Healing of Consciousness"
David Frawley and Vasant Lad: "The Yoga of Herbs: An Ayurvedic Guide to Herbal Medicine"
M.D. Deepak Chopra: "Perfect Health: The Complete Mind/Body Guide, Revised and Updated Edition"